PROBLEMS
IN MECHANICS

Professor of Engineering Science
University of California, Berkeley

George Leitmann

Professor of Applied Mechanics
University of California, Berkeley

Werner Goldsmith

McGraw-Hill Book Company

New York   San Francisco   St. Louis   Toronto   London   Sydney

PROBLEMS IN MECHANICS

Printed in the United States of America.

Library of Congress catalog card number: 68–17191

37152

1234567890 HOCZ 7543210698

PREFACE

This collection of problems is intended for use in an introductory course in engineering mechanics (statics and dynamics of particles, systems of particles, and rigid bodies) in conjunction with an appropriate text. In particular, the coverage and sequence of subject matter is arranged to correspond to Parts 1 and 2 of Synge and Griffith, *Principles of Mechanics*, 3d edition, McGraw-Hill Book Company, New York, 1959. Part 1 deals with motion in the plane; Part 2 deals with three-dimensional motion.

Most sections are introduced by one or more sample problems. The solutions to these problems are presented in full; they employ the methods discussed by Synge and Griffith in the corresponding sections of the text, except for the use of vector operations (scalar and vector product) throughout the volume.

The compilers of this collection are grateful to their students and colleagues for suggesting problems. They are expecially indebted to Professor C. P. Atkinson for a number of problems in the early sections.

George Leitmann
Werner Goldsmith

iii

CONTENTS

Preface   *iii*

CHAPTER 1   **FOUNDATIONS OF MECHANICS**   **2**
              1.3   Introduction to vectors. Velocity and acceleration   *2*
              1.4   Fundamental laws of Newtonian mechanics   *7*
              1.5   The theory of dimensions   *10*

CHAPTER 2   **METHODS OF PLANE STATICS**   **12**
              2.2   Equilibrium of a particle   *12*
              2.3   Equilibrium of a system of particles   *16*
              2.4   Work and potential energy   *23*

CHAPTER 3   **APPLICATIONS IN PLANE STATICS**   **30**
              3.1   Mass centers and centers of gravity   *30*
              3.2   Friction   *36*
              3.3   Thin beams   *41*
              3.4   Flexible cables   *44*
              3.5   Frames   *48*

CHAPTER 4   **PLANE KINEMATICS**   **60**
              4.1   Kinematics of a particle   *60*
              4.2   Motion of a rigid body parallel to a fixed plane   *65*

iv   Contents

CHAPTER 5   METHODS OF PLANE DYNAMICS   70
             5.1 Motion of a particle   70
             5.2 Motion of a system   75
             5.3 Moving frames of reference   81

CHAPTER 6   APPLICATIONS IN PLANE DYNAMICS: MOTION OF A
             PARTICLE   88
             6.1 Projectiles without resistance   88
             6.2 Projectiles with resistance   92
             6.3 Harmonic oscillators   95
             6.4 General motion under a central force   107
             6.5 Planetary orbits   110

CHAPTER 7   APPLICATIONS IN A PLANE DYNAMICS: MOTION OF A
             RIGID BODY AND OF A SYSTEM   116
             7.1 Moments of inertia. Kinetic energy and angular momentum   116
             7.2 Rigid body rotating about a fixed axis   121
             7.3 General motion of a rigid body parallel to a fixed plane   125
             7.4 Normal modes of vibration   131
             7.5 Stability of equilibrium   134

CHAPTER 8   PLANE IMPULSIVE MOTION   138
             8.1 General theory of plane impulsive motion   138
             8.2 Collisions   140
             8.3 Applications   142

v   Contents

CHAPTER **9**   **PRODUCTS OF VECTORS**   **146**

9.1   *The scalar and vector products*   *146*
9.2   *Triple products*   *148*
9.3   *Moments of vectors*   *150*

CHAPTER **10**   **STATICS IN SPACE**   **152**

10.1 *General force systems*   *152*
10.2 *Equilibrium of a system of particles*   *154*
10.3 *Reduction of force systems*   *157*
10.4 *Equilibrium of a rigid body*   *163*
10.5 *Displacements of a rigid body*   *172*
10.6 *Generalized coordinates and constraints*   *174*
10.7 *Work and potential energy*   *178*

CHAPTER **11**   **KINEMATICS: KINETIC ENERGY AND ANGULAR
                   MOMENTUM**   **186**

11.1 *Kinematics of a particle*   *186*
11.2 *Kinematics of a rigid body*   *189*
11.3 *Moments and products of inertia*   *194*
11.4 *Kinetic energy*   *201*
11.5 *Angular momentum*   *205*

vi   *Contents*

CHAPTER 12   **METHODS OF DYNAMICS IN SPACE**   **208**

         12.1 Motion of a particle   *208*
         12.2 Motion of a system   *212*
         12.3 Moving frames of reference   *217*
         12.4 Motion of a rigid body   *221*
         12.5 Impulsive motion   *227*

CHAPTER 13   **APPLICATIONS IN DYNAMICS IN SPACE: MOTION OF A PARTICLE**   **232**

         13.2 The simple pendulum   *232*
         13.3 The spherical pendulum   *234*
         13.4 The motion of a charged particle in an electromagnetic field   *236*
         13.5 Effects of the earth's rotation   *237*

CHAPTER 14   **APPLICATIONS IN DYNAMICS IN SPACE: MOTION OF A RIGID BODY**   **240**

         14.1 Motion of a rigid body with a fixed point under no forces   *240*
         14.2 The spinning top   *242*
         14.3 Gyroscopes   *244*
         14.4 General motion of a rigid body   *246*

vii   Contents

Problems
in Mechanics

FOUNDATIONS
OF MECHANICS

Section 1.3   Introduction to vectors.
Velocity and acceleration

SAMPLE PROBLEM   A unit vector **e** rotates in a plane with angular velocity $\omega = \dot{\theta}\mathbf{k}$ relative to triad **ijk**. Show that the time derivative $\dot{\mathbf{e}}$ of **e** is a vector in the **ij**-plane normal to **e**.

Solution

Since

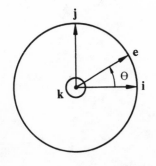

$$\mathbf{e} = \mathbf{i} \cos \theta + \mathbf{j} \sin \theta$$

we have

$$\dot{\mathbf{e}} = (-\mathbf{i} \sin \theta + \mathbf{j} \cos \theta)\dot{\theta}$$

Hence

$$\mathbf{e} \cdot \dot{\mathbf{e}} = 0$$

so that $\dot{\mathbf{e}}$ is perpendicular to **e**. Furthermore, the vector $\mathbf{e}_\theta = (-\mathbf{i} \sin \theta + \mathbf{j} \cos \theta)$ is a unit vector. Thus we may write

$$\dot{\mathbf{e}} = \mathbf{e}_\theta \dot{\theta}$$

CHAPTER 1

Given an orthogonal triad of unit vectors **ijk**, express the position vectors $\mathbf{r}_A$ and $\mathbf{r}_B$ with respect to the origin for the points $A(3,-2,5)$ and $B(1,4,-2)$. What is the position of B with respect to A?

A force $\mathbf{F} = 5\mathbf{i} + 6\mathbf{j} - 3\mathbf{k}$ lb has a line of action through point $(1,2,3)$. Find the direction cosines of the force. What is the component of the force $\mathbf{F}$ along the unit vector $\mathbf{i}$; $\mathbf{j}$; $\mathbf{k}$?

A vector starts at the origin and extends outward through the point $(4,-1,3)$ to a total length of 10 units. Give an expression for the vector and determine its direction cosines.

The sum of the two vectors $\mathbf{P}$ and $\mathbf{Q}$ is given by

$$\mathbf{R} = \mathbf{P} + \mathbf{Q}$$

If $\mathbf{P} = 30\mathbf{i} + 40\mathbf{j}$ and $\mathbf{Q} = 20\mathbf{i} - 20\mathbf{j}$, find the vector $\mathbf{R}$. What angle does $\mathbf{R}$ make with the direction of the unit vector $\mathbf{i}$?

PROBLEM 1.3.5 Given: $\mathbf{P} = 30\mathbf{i} + 40\mathbf{j} - 7\mathbf{k}$

$$\mathbf{Q} = 6\mathbf{i} - 5\mathbf{j}$$

Determine: (a) $\mathbf{P} + \mathbf{Q}$

(b) $\mathbf{P} - \mathbf{Q}$

(c) $\mathbf{P} \cdot \mathbf{Q}$

(d) $(\mathbf{P} + \mathbf{Q}) \cdot (\mathbf{P} - \mathbf{Q})$

PROBLEM 1.3.6 Show that the angle θ between the two vectors $\mathbf{A}$ and $\mathbf{B}$ is given by

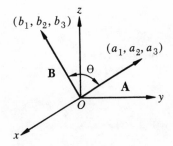

$$\cos \theta = \frac{a_1 b_1 + a_2 b_2 + a_3 b_3}{(a_1^2 + a_2^2 + a_3^2)(b_1^2 + b_2^2 + b_3^2)}$$

where a_1, a_2, a_3 and b_1, b_2, b_3 are the direction cosines of $\mathbf{A}$ and $\mathbf{B}$, respectively.

PROBLEM 1.3.7 Given a vector $\overrightarrow{PQ}$ defined by the line segment beginning at point $P(-3,1,5)$ and terminating at $Q(4,0,-2)$, express $\overrightarrow{PQ}$ in terms of unit vectors directed along the rectangular Cartesian coordinate axes. Find the component of $\overrightarrow{PQ}$ in the direction defined by a line passing through the points $(3,1,-1)$ and $(-1,2,7)$.

PROBLEM 1.3.8 For the right-handed rectangular triad $\mathbf{ijk}$, show that

$$\mathbf{A} \times \mathbf{B} = \begin{vmatrix} \mathbf{i} & \mathbf{j} & \mathbf{k} \\ a_1 & a_2 & a_3 \\ b_1 & b_2 & b_3 \end{vmatrix}$$

where $\mathbf{A} = a_1\mathbf{i} + a_2\mathbf{j} + a_3\mathbf{k}$

$$\mathbf{B} = b_1\mathbf{i} + b_2\mathbf{j} + b_3\mathbf{k}$$

4

For the right-handed rectangular triad **ijk**, show that the   **PROBLEM 1.3.9**
triple cross product $\mathbf{i} \times (\mathbf{i} \times \mathbf{j}) = -\mathbf{j}$.

Show that the time derivative of the vector $\dot{\mathbf{e}}$ of the sample   **PROBLEM 1.3.10**
problem at the beginning of this section can be represented
by the vector $-\omega^2\mathbf{e}$, if $\dot{\theta} = \omega$ is constant.

A velocity vector is given by the following expression: **PROBLEM 1.3.11**

$$\mathbf{v}(t) = 2t^2\mathbf{i} + (3t^3 - 1)\mathbf{j} - (t - t^4)\mathbf{k} \qquad \text{ft/sec}$$

Find the acceleration vector as a function of time t. What is
the acceleration at $t = 2$ sec?

A particle, located at the point $(0,1,-1)$ at time $t = 0$, moves   **PROBLEM 1.3.12**
in a straight line and with a constant speed of 3 ft/sec toward
the point $(-1,3,1)$. Find the velocity and the position vector
of the particle. (Note: Coordinates are given in ft.)

The velocity **v** of a particle is given as   **PROBLEM 1.3.13**

$$\mathbf{v} = \frac{d\mathbf{r}}{dt} = 6\cos 3t\mathbf{i} + 4t^3\mathbf{j} - \sin 3t\mathbf{k}$$

At $t = 0$, $\mathbf{r}(0) = \mathbf{i} + \mathbf{j} + \mathbf{k}$.

(a) Find the position vector $\mathbf{r}(t)$.
(b) Find the acceleration of the particle as a function of time.

Introduction to vectors. Velocity and acceleration   5

PROBLEM 1.3.14 Show that

(a) $\dfrac{d}{dt}(c\mathbf{A}) = \dfrac{dc}{dt}\mathbf{A} + c\,\dfrac{d\mathbf{A}}{dt}$

(b) $\dfrac{d}{dt}(\mathbf{A} \cdot \mathbf{B}) = \dfrac{d\mathbf{A}}{dt}\cdot\mathbf{B} + \mathbf{A}\cdot\dfrac{d\mathbf{B}}{dt}$

(c) $\dfrac{d}{dt}(\mathbf{A} \times \mathbf{B}) = \dfrac{d\mathbf{A}}{dt}\times\mathbf{B} + \mathbf{A}\times\dfrac{d\mathbf{B}}{dt}.$

where $\mathbf{A} = a_1\mathbf{i} + a_2\mathbf{j} + a_3\mathbf{k}$

$\mathbf{B} = b_1\mathbf{i} + b_2\mathbf{j} + b_3\mathbf{k}$

and where c, a_i, b_i ($i = 1, 2, 3$) are functions of t.

PROBLEM 1.3.15 Find the gradient of each of the following scalar functions of x, y, and z:

(a) $V = 6x + 9y - 6z$

(b) $V = -Ax^4y$

(c) $V = Axy + Byz + Cxz$

where A, B, and C are constants.

PROBLEM 1.3.16 Find the gradient of the function

$$V = (\mathbf{A} \cdot \mathbf{B}) \qquad \text{at the point } (1, -1, 2)$$

where $\mathbf{A} = xy\mathbf{i} + yz\mathbf{j} + zx\mathbf{k}$

$\mathbf{B} = y\mathbf{i} + z\mathbf{j} + x\mathbf{k}$

PROBLEM 1.3.17 The position of a particle as a function of time t is given by

$$\mathbf{r} = t^3\mathbf{i} + 6t\mathbf{k} \times \left(\frac{t^2}{6}\mathbf{j} - t^2\mathbf{i}\right)$$

Determine the velocity and acceleration at $t = 1$.

6

A person traveling due north at a speed of 15 mph notices the apparent direction of the wind to be from the west. He doubles his speed and observes that the apparent direction of the wind is from the northwest. Find the direction and speed of the wind relative to the earth.

Section 1.4 Fundamental laws of Newtonian mechanics

Newton's law of universal gravitation states that the magni- tude of the attractive force between two particles of masses m_A and m_B, respectively, is

$$|\mathbf{F}| = \frac{Gm_A m_B}{r^2}$$

where the universal gravitational constant

$$G = 3.41 \times 10^{-8} \text{ ft}^3/\text{slug-sec}^2$$

and r is the distance between the particles.

It can be shown (see Sec. 3.1 of Synge and Griffith) that the attractive force exerted by a spherically symmetrical body is the same as that due to a particle of equal mass located at the center of the body. Neglecting the rotation of the attracting body, the attractive force is the weight of the attracted body.

If a particle of mass m_B situated at the surface of the earth (treated as a spherically symmetrical body) has a weight of magnitude $m_B g$, where the mass of the earth $m_E = 4.12 \times 10^{23}$ slugs and the radius of the earth $r_E = 3,960$ miles, determine the acceleration of gravity g at the surface of the earth.

Solution

$$|\mathbf{F}| = m_B g = \frac{Gm_E m_B}{r_E^2} = 32.2 m_B \text{ lb}$$

$$g = 32.2 \text{ ft/sec}^2$$

A man weighs 200 lb at sea level. How much does he weigh at an altitude of 500 miles above sea level? Assume the radius of the earth $r_E = 3,960$ miles.

PROBLEM 1.4.2 A man weighs 200 lb at the surface of the earth. How much would he weigh at the surface of the moon? The mass of the earth is 81 times the mass of the moon, and the radius of the earth is $\frac{11}{3}$ the radius of the moon. Neglect the gravitational attraction of the earth on the man at the moon.

PROBLEM 1.4.3 Suppose that in the sample problem at the beginning of this section the universal gravitational constant is given as

$$G = 6.67 \times 10^{-8} \text{ cm}^3/\text{g-sec}^2$$

the mass of the earth is given as

$$m_E = 5.98 \times 10^{27} \text{ g}$$

and the radius of the earth is given as

$$r_E = 6.38 \times 10^8 \text{ cm}$$

What is the magnitude of the acceleration of gravity at the surface of the earth in cm/sec^2?

PROBLEM 1.4.4 Find the resultant of the coplanar forces acting on the particle P shown.

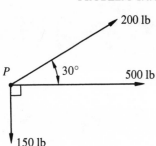

PROBLEM 1.4.5 A force $\mathbf{F} = 5\mathbf{i} + 6\mathbf{j} - 3\mathbf{k}$ lb acts on a particle of mass 2 slugs. What are the components of the acceleration vector in the $\mathbf{i},\mathbf{j},\mathbf{k}$ directions?

PROBLEM 1.4.6 The position vector of a particle of mass 5 slugs relative to Newtonian frame $\mathbf{ijk}$ is

$$\mathbf{r} = (1 - 2t^2)\mathbf{i} + 2t^3\mathbf{j} + (5t^2 - t)\mathbf{k} \text{ ft}$$

Find the force acting on the particle at time $t = 2$ sec.

Foundations of mechanics

If the velocity vector of a particle of mass $m = 5$ units is

$$\mathbf{v}(t) = 6 \cos 2t\mathbf{i} + 2t^2\mathbf{j} - 6 \sin 2t\mathbf{k} \text{ units}$$

where **ijk** is a Newtonian frame, find the force acting on the particle at $t = 2$ sec if
(a) **v** has units of centimeters per second and the mass is in grams,
(b) **v** has units of feet per second and the mass is in slugs,
(c) **v** has units of meters per second and the mass is in kilograms.

A horizontal 5-lb force is applied to a block which weighs 10 lb and rests on a horizontal frictionless table. What is the resulting acceleration of the block?

Two objects weighing 300 and 200 lb, respectively, are attached to opposite ends of a light inextensible string passing over a light frictionless pulley. Find the acceleration of each object and the tension in the string.

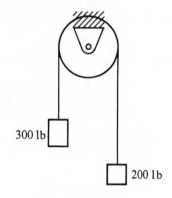

300 lb

200 lb

Blocks A and B weighing 40 and 15 lb, respectively, are connected by a rope passing over a pulley as shown. Find the acceleration of block B. Neglect the mass of the rope and pulley as well as all friction.

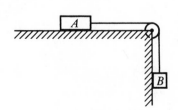

Fundamental laws of Newtonian mechanics

PROBLEM 1.4.11 Blocks A and B weighing 35 and 70 lb, respectively, are connected by a rope passing over a pulley as shown. Find the acceleration of block A. Assume that the rope is weightless, flexible, and inextensible and that the pulley is frictionless and of negligible mass. The surfaces are smooth.

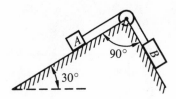

PROBLEM 1.4.12 The 150- and 100-lb weights are attached to the rope passing over the pulleys as shown. Assume that the pulleys are massless and frictionless and that the rope is weightless, flexible, and inextensible. Find the accelerations of each weight and the tension in the rope.

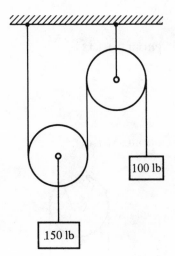

Section 1.5 The theory of dimensions

PROBLEM 1.5.1 In the cgs system of units, the unit of force is the dyne. Express the gravitational force in dynes exerted on a man weighing 150 lb at the surface of the earth. What is the force in poundals?

PROBLEM 1.5.2 What acceleration will a 10-kg mass have when acted on by a force $\mathbf{F} = 3\mathbf{i} + 2\mathbf{j} + \mathbf{k}$ newtons? Express the acceleration also in cm/sec^2.

A body weighs 10 lb. What force is required to impart an
acceleration of 10 ft/sec^2 to the body? Express the force in
dynes.

Two positive static charges Q_1 and Q_2 at rest in a vacuum
are a distance R in. apart. The force on Q_2 due to Q_1 is

$$\mathbf{F}_{21} = k\frac{Q_1 Q_2}{R^2}\mathbf{e}_R$$

where $\mathbf{e}_R$ is a unit vector directed along the line connecting
Q_1 with Q_2, and k is a dimensionless constant.
(a) What is the force on Q_1 due to Q_2?
(b) What must be the dimension of the charge in this
particular system of units?

METHODS
OF PLANE STATICS

Section 2.2   Equilibrium of a particle

A 500-lb weight is attached to a 50-ft rope. A man at A pushes the weight out over the edge of a roof so that the rope makes an angle of 10° with the vertical.

Find the necessary force **F** and the tension in the rope to keep the weight at rest in the position shown. Neglect the weight of the rope.

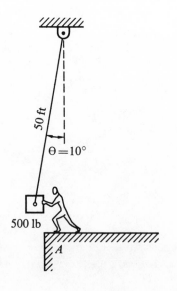

50 ft

$\theta = 10°$

500 lb

A

CHAPTER 2

Solution

Free-body diagram:

$$\Sigma F_V = 0: \qquad T\cos\theta = 500$$

$$\Sigma F_H = 0: \qquad F = T\sin\theta$$

So

$$T = \frac{500}{\cos 10°} = 507 \text{ lb}$$

$$F = 500 \tan 10° = 88 \text{ lb}$$

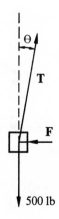

PROBLEM 2.2.1 A block weighing 100 lb is supported by two cables as shown. Find the tension in each of the two cables.

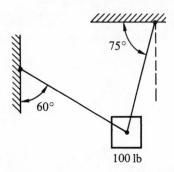

PROBLEM 2.2.2 Find the vertical force **P** required to maintain the system shown in equilibrium. Neglect friction.

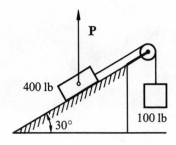

PROBLEM 2.2.3 A ring of weight W is constrained to move along a circular wire in the vertical plane. A string passing over a small pulley at C connects a body of weight P to the ring. Find the relation between P, W, and θ for equilibrium. Neglect friction at the pulley and between the ring and wire.

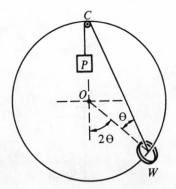

A bead B weighing $\frac{1}{2}$ lb rests in a smooth semicircular bowl of radius $R = 6$ in. The bead is kept in equilibrium by a light inextensible string AB attached to a fixed support at a distance of 4 in. above the rim of the bowl as shown. Determine the tension in the string.

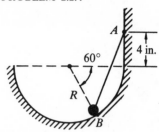

A small sphere A of weight 2 lb is constrained to move in a smooth vertical tube. A linear spring AB of spring constant $k = 1.5$ lb/in. and free length $L = 6$ in. has end B fixed as shown and is attached to the sphere through a slot in the tube. Determine the equilibrium position (angle θ) of the sphere and the corresponding spring force.

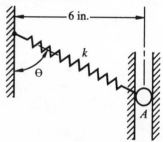

A small block B weighing 5 lb is held in equilibrium under the action of a light string AB of length L and a linear spring BC as shown. If the free length of the spring is $1.5L$, determine the required spring constant.

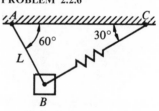

What force must the man at A exert to keep the system in the position shown? The strings are light and inextensible, and the system is frictionless. Neglect the mass of the pulleys.

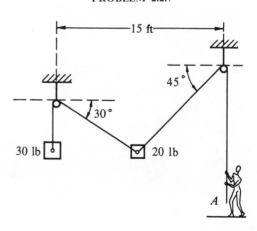

Section 2.3 Equilibrium of a system of particles

Replace the loading shown by the resultant **F** acting at point A and a couple of moment **M**.

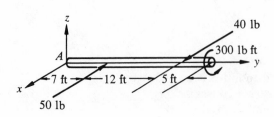

Solution

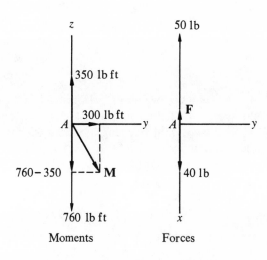

$$\mathbf{M} = \sum_{i=1}^{3} \mathbf{M}_i = 300\mathbf{j} + (7\mathbf{j} \times (-50)\mathbf{i}) + (19\mathbf{j} \times 40\mathbf{i})$$

$$= 300\mathbf{j} + 350\mathbf{k} - 760\mathbf{k} = 300\mathbf{j} - 410\mathbf{k} \text{ lb-ft}$$

$$|\mathbf{M}| = \sqrt{(300)^2 + (410)^2} = 508 \text{ lb-ft}$$

$$\mathbf{F} = \sum_{i=1}^{2} \mathbf{F}_i = (-50)\mathbf{i} + (40)\mathbf{i} = -10\mathbf{i} \text{ lb}$$

$$|\mathbf{F}| = 10 \text{ lb}$$

Methods of plane statics

A 50-lb wheel rests against a step as shown. Determine the couple C which will just lift the wheel off the floor. Assume no slipping at edge A.

PROBLEM 2.3.1

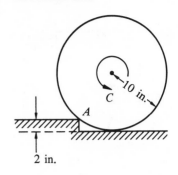

Determine the single force equipollent to the force system acting on the frame shown. Neglecting the weight of the members, is the frame in equilibrium under the applied force system?

PROBLEM 2.3.2

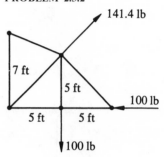

A uniform beam AB of weight W and length L rests with one end against a smooth vertical wall and the other end on smooth horizontal ground as shown. Slipping is prevented by a string BC extending horizontally from the foot of the beam to the foot of the wall.

Find the tension in the string and the forces exerted on the beam by the ground and wall in terms of W and θ.

PROBLEM 2.3.3

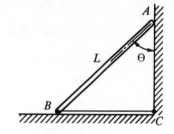

Find the moments about the z-axis of the following forces in the xy-plane:

PROBLEM 2.3.4

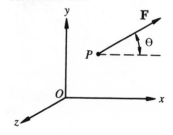

Magnitude of **F**	Angle θ	Coordinates of P
30 lb	45°	(5,4,0) ft
5 dynes	60°	(1,6,0) cm
100 newtons	300°	(−4,3,0) m

PROBLEM 2.3.5   If the combined moment about the z-axis of the two coplanar forces shown is 320 lb-ft clockwise and their resultant is a 150-lb force, find $|\mathbf{F}|$ and θ.

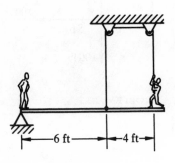

PROBLEM 2.3.6   A 150-lb man supports himself on a uniform 50-lb beam by means of a light rope stretched over two frictionless pulleys as shown.

(a)   What tension must the man exert on the rope to hold himself in equilibrium?

(b)   How far out on the beam can his 150-lb colleague go before equilibrium is lost?

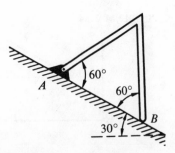

PROBLEM 2.3.7   The rigid uniform frame shown in the figure is pinned at A and supported by the smooth surface at B. The frame weighs 50 lb. Find the reaction at A

(a) by solving the equilibrium equations;

(b) by a graphical method.

18   *Methods of plane statics*

Find the magnitude of force **P** to just lift the 80-lb roller off the incline when $\theta = 20°$. Assume no slipping at A and neglect the weight of the bar. Also find the least value of $|\mathbf{P}|$ and the corresponding angle θ to accomplish the task.

PROBLEM 2.3.8

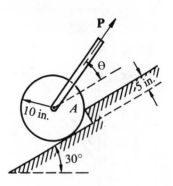

A vertical mast of weight Q guided at A and B is kept in equilibrium by the roller support C as shown. Neglecting friction at the guides, determine the reactions at A, B, and C.

PROBLEM 2.3.9

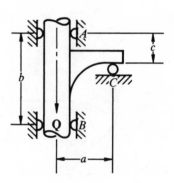

Find the forces in the hinged bars AD, AE, and BC supporting the horizontal beam AB on which the concentrated vertical load **P** and a couple G are acting. Neglect the weights of the beam and bars.

PROBLEM 2.3.10

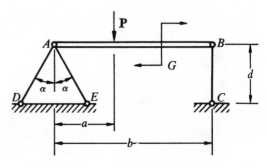

Equilibrium of a system of particles   19

PROBLEM 2.3.11

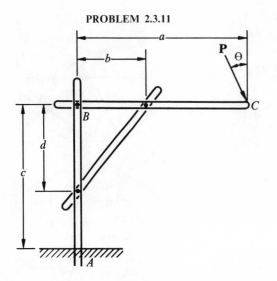

The pinned structure of negligible weight is anchored in a cement foundation at A and carries a load P inclined at an angle θ to the vertical as shown. Determine the reaction at A.

PROBLEM 2.3.12

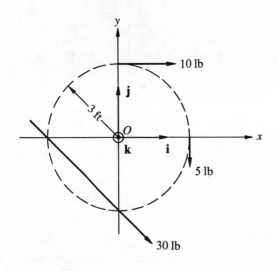

Replace the plane force system acting on a rigid body shown in the figure by an equipollent system with a force acting through O. Express the equipollent system in terms of i,j,k components.

PROBLEM 2.3.13 Find the system with the resultant force passing through point $(0,0)$ which is equipollent to a system composed of the three forces: $F_1 = -200i$ through point $(2,3)$, $F_2 = 100i + 200j$ through $(0,1)$, and $F_3 = 100j$ through $(2,3)$.

Methods of plane statics

Find the magnitude and direction of the force **F** that makes the coplanar force system shown equipollent to a couple.

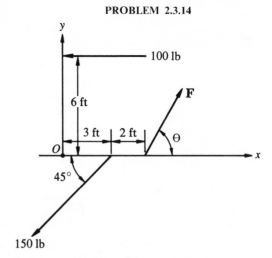

Replace the parallel force system shown by an equipollent system with a resultant force passing through the origin O. Show that the system is also equipollent to a single force acting at a distance d from the origin, and determine d.

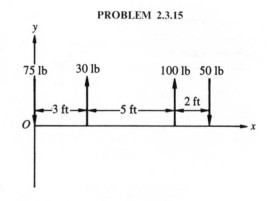

The bell crank shown is acted upon by a 200-lb-in. couple, two forces at C, and a linear spring at A. Determine the spring force necessary to hold the system in equilibrium. Neglect the weight of the bell crank.

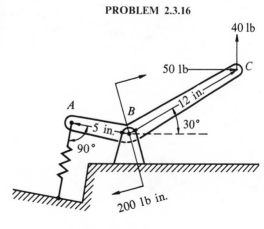

Equilibrium of a system of particles

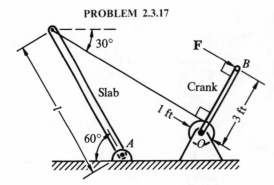

A uniform concrete slab of length $l = 5$ ft and weight $w = 1,000$ lb is pinned at A and is held in the position shown by a light cable. The cable drum has a diameter of 1 ft. Find the magnitude of the force F required to hold the slab in equilibrium. Neglect friction and the weight of arm OB.

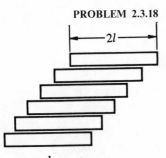

A child has a large supply of identical uniform blocks, each of weight W and length $2l$. He piles them on top of one another with a certain overhang that may vary from block to block.
(a) Show that with the proper overhang of each block over the one below it, the child can build a structure that overhangs the base by any distance desired.
(b) What is the minimum height of the pile for a 25-in. overhang, if each block has a thickness of 2 in. and a length $2l = 8$ in.

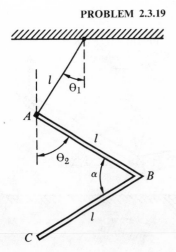

Two prismatic bars AB and BC, each of length l and weight W, are rigidly joined at B and suspended in a vertical plane by a light string of length l as shown in the figure. Determine the angles θ_1 and θ_2 for equilibrium.

Methods of plane statics

A uniform T-shaped bar of weight $W = 10$ lb and members of equal length $l = 4$ ft is suspended in the vertical plane by a smooth pin as shown. What is angle θ when the bar is held in equilibrium under the action of a vertical force $\mathbf{P} = 10$ lb at B?

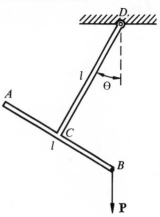

Section 2.4   Work and potential energy

Uniform bars AB and AC, each of weight W and length L, are connected by a smooth pin at A. Bar AB is attached to a frictionless pin at B, while bar AC is pinned to a light frictionless roller at C. The system is in equilibrium when a horizontal force $\mathbf{P}$ is applied at C. Find the angle θ by the method of virtual work.

SAMPLE PROBLEM

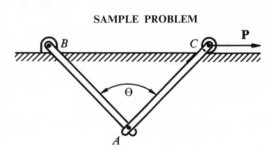

Solution

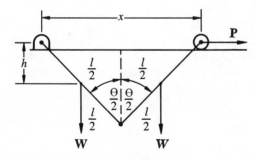

Work and potential energy

$$\delta(\text{Work}) = P\,\delta x + W\,\delta h = 0$$

$$h = \frac{l}{2}\cos\frac{\theta}{2} \qquad \delta h = -\frac{l}{4}\sin\frac{\theta}{2}\,\delta\theta$$

$$x = 2l\sin\frac{\theta}{2} \qquad \delta x = l\cos\frac{\theta}{2}\,\delta\theta$$

$$Pl\cos\frac{\theta}{2}\,\delta\theta - 2W\,\frac{l}{4}\sin\frac{\theta}{2}\,\delta\theta = 0$$

or

$$P\cos\frac{\theta}{2} = \frac{W\sin(\theta/2)}{2}$$

$$\frac{1}{2}\theta = \tan^{-1}\frac{2P}{W}$$

PROBLEM 2.4.1 A uniform bar of weight W and length l can rotate freely about a fixed pin at end A. End B is attached to a string which passes over a small pulley at C located a distance h directly above A. A block of weight W, equal to that of the bar, is tied to the end of the string. Determine the equilibrium configuration by the method of virtual work.

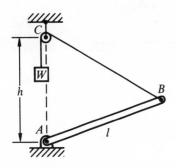

PROBLEM 2.4.2 Two wheels of weights W_1 and W_2, respectively, and each of radius R, are pinned to a weightless bar of length l. The system is placed on the triangular support shown. Neglecting friction, determine the distance x when the system is in equilibrium. Use the method of virtual work.

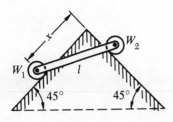

A rod of length l and weight W can slide on a smooth hemispherical track of radius R, with $2R > l$. The rod is non-uniform and has its center of gravity C at a distance $l/4$ from one end. What is the angle θ between the bar and the horizontal when the bar is in equilibrium? Use the method of virtual work.

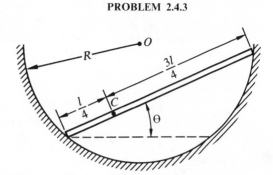

Two weightless bars AD and BC, each of length $2b$, are pinned together at their centers E. Each bar is pinned to a weightless roller resting on a horizontal surface and carries a weight W at its upper end. Ends A and B are connected by a linear spring with constant k and free length b. Use the virtual work method to determine the angle θ for equilibrium. Neglect friction at pins C, D, and E.

Two light wheels of radii r_1 and r_2, respectively, are rigidly joined to form the pulley shown in the figure. What is the force **P** that maintains the load Q in equilibrium? Use the method of virtual work.

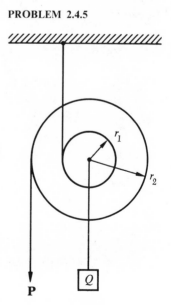

PROBLEM 2.4.6 A mass m on a smooth horizontal surface is attached to a fixed support by means of a non-linear spring. The potential energy of the system is

$$V = \tfrac{1}{2}kx^2 + \tfrac{1}{4}bx^4$$

where k and b are constants and x is the distance from the equilibrium position. Find the force exerted by the spring.

PROBLEM 2.4.7 A uniform rod of length l and weight W is supported by a smooth peg and vertical wall as shown. What is the relation between dimension a and rod length l in order that equilibrium be possible? Using the method of virtual work, determine angle θ at equilibrium.

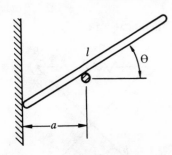

PROBLEM 2.4.8 The potential energy V of a conservative system is given by

$$V = \frac{ax^2}{2} + \frac{bx^3}{3}$$

where a and b are constants. Determine the value(s) of coordinate x at equilibrium.

PROBLEM 2.4.9 A two-dimensional force field

$$\mathbf{F} = -\,\mathrm{grad}\ V(x,y)$$

is conservative if and only if

$$\frac{\partial^2 V}{\partial x\,\partial y} = \frac{\partial^2 V}{\partial y\,\partial z}$$

What is the analogous relation if the function V is expressed in polar coordinates, that is, $V(r,\theta)$?

PROBLEM 2.4.10 Find the work done by the following forces around the closed path corresponding to straight lines (0,0) to (1,0), (1,0) to (1,2), and (1,2) to (0,0):

26

(a) $\mathbf{F} = 2x^2\mathbf{i} - 3y^2\mathbf{j}$ lb $(x,y$ in ft$)$
(b) $\mathbf{F} = Axy\mathbf{i} + Bx^2\mathbf{j}$ dynes $(x,y$ in cm$)$
(c) $\mathbf{F} = 2x\mathbf{i} + 5y\mathbf{j}$ newtons $(x,y$ in m$)$

Two light bars AB and CB each of length l are pinned to each other at B. Bar AB is pinned to a fixed support at A, and bar CB is pinned at C to a light roller resting on a plane surface. A force $\mathbf{F}$ parallel to the surface is applied at C. The bars are connected by a linear spring of stiffness k as shown. The spring exerts no force on the bars when $x = a$. Determine the distance x for equilibrium. Neglect friction at pins A, B, and C.

PROBLEM 2.4.11

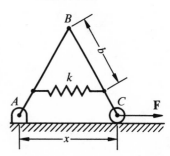

Collar A, supported by a linear spring of constant k, can slide on the vertical shaft without friction. Rod BC of length l is pinned at its center to collar A and at end C to rod CD of length $l/2$. Rod CD is pinned at D to the fixed shaft. A ball of weight W is attached at B to rod BC. The spring is unstressed when $\theta = \pi/2$. Determine the angle θ at equilibrium. Neglect the weights of the rods as well as friction at the pins.

PROBLEM 2.4.12

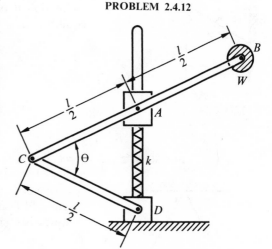

The three circular cylinders, shown in cross section, are in equilibrium. Cylinders 1 and 2 weigh 100 lb each and are 4 in. in diameter. Cylinder 3 weighs 200 lb and has a 6-in. diameter. Determine the reactions at A, B, C, D, E, and F. Neglect friction.

PROBLEM 2.4.13

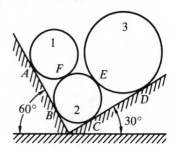

Work and potential energy   27

PROBLEM 2.4.14 Find the force fields associated with the following potential energy functions:

(a) $V = -5x + 10y - 8z$ ft-lb
(b) $V = 2x^2y - 3y^2x$ dyne-cm
(c) $V = \dfrac{x}{y} + \dfrac{y}{x}$ ft-lb
(d) $V = \mu/r$ newton-m; $\mu = $ const
(e) $V = mg$ ft-lb; $mg = $ const

PROBLEM 2.4.15 A uniform bar of length l and weight w rests with its lower end in contact with a smooth vertical wall. The bar passes over a smooth peg at A a distance c from the wall and carries a weight W suspended from its upper end. Find the inclination θ of the bar to the vertical when the bar is in equilibrium.

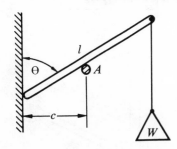

PROBLEM 2.4.16 A weightless strut AB, 2 ft long, is hung from support C by means of two light strings, each of length 2 ft. A 50-lb weight is suspended at D by means of two light strings, each of length 2 ft. Use the method of virtual work to determine the compressive force in the strut.

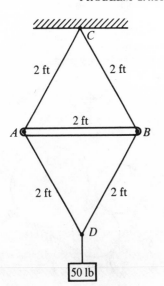

28

Two uniform rods AB and BC of weights W_1 and W_2, respectively, are pinned to each other at B. Rod AB is pinned to a fixed support at A. A horizontal force $\mathbf{P}$ is applied at C. Neglecting friction, show that for equilibrium

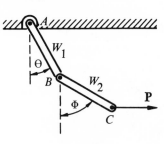

$$\tan \theta = \frac{2P}{W_1 + 2W_2} \qquad \tan \phi = \frac{2P}{W_2}$$

APPLICATIONS
IN PLANE STATICS

Section 3.1   Mass centers
and centers of gravity

Locate the center of mass C of a homogeneous hemispherical shell of radius r and negligible wall thickness.

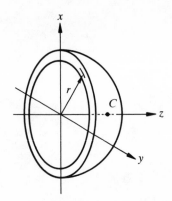

Solution

The problem is equivalent to finding the centroid C of the surface of a hemisphere, since the shell is homogeneous and of negligible thickness. From symmetry we note that $\bar{x} = \bar{y} = 0$.

CHAPTER 3

The element of length of the intersection of the surface with the (xz)-plane is given by

$$ds = \sqrt{1 + \left(\frac{dx}{dz}\right)^2}\, dz$$

An element of surface area is

$$dA = 2\pi \times ds = 2\pi \times \left[1 + \left(\frac{dx}{dz}\right)^2\right]^{1/2} dz$$

$$= 2\pi \times \left(1 + \frac{z^2}{x^2}\right)^{1/2} dz = 2\pi r\, dz$$

Then by definition

$$\bar{z} = \frac{\int z\, dA}{\int dA} = \frac{\displaystyle\int_0^r 2\pi r z\, dz}{\displaystyle\int_0^r 2\pi r\, dz} = \frac{1}{2}z\Big|_0^r = \frac{1}{2}r$$

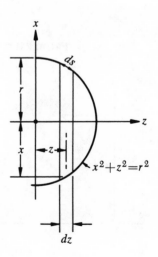

$x^2 + z^2 = r^2$

PROBLEM 3.1.1 Show that the center of mass of a thin homogeneous sheet in the shape of a circular sector is given by

$$\bar{x} = 0 \qquad \bar{y} = \frac{2}{3}\frac{r \sin \theta}{\theta}$$

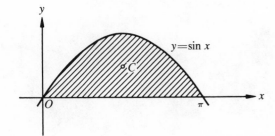

PROBLEM 3.1.2

Locate the centroid C of the area bounded by the curve $y = \sin x$ and the x-axis for $0 \leqslant x \leqslant \pi$.

$y = \sin x$

PROBLEM 3.1.3 Find the center of mass of the thin homogeneous wire bent in the shape of a parabolic arc extending from $x = 0$ to $x = 1$, defined by the equation $y^2 = 4x$.

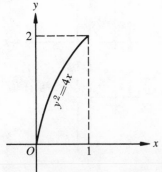

Applications in plane statics

Find the center of mass of a rectangular parallelepiped of a
spongy material whose density ρ varies directly with height
according to the formula

$$\rho = \rho_0(z_0 - z) \qquad \text{where } \rho_0 = \text{const}$$

PROBLEM 3.1.4

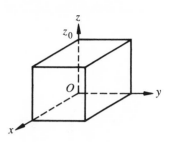

Locate the center of mass C of the thin plate bounded by the
curve $y = \cos x$, the y-axis and the x-axis for $0 \leqslant x \leqslant \pi/2$.
The density ρ of the plate varies linearly in the y-direction
according to the relation $\rho = 0.1 + 0.01y$.

PROBLEM 3.1.5

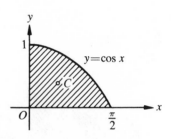

Find the center of mass of the solid cylinder
of radius a and length l. The density ρ of
the cylinder varies as a function of y according to:

$$\rho = K(1 + y) \qquad \text{where } K = \text{const}$$

PROBLEM 3.1.6

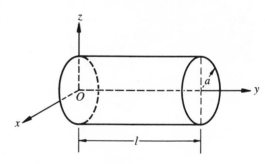

Locate the center of mass of the homogeneous thin rod shown in the figure.

PROBLEM 3.1.7

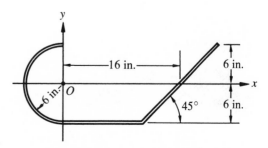

Mass centers and centers of gravity

PROBLEM 3.1.8

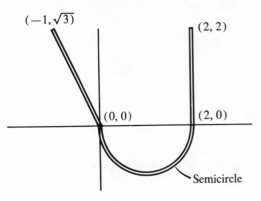

Find the center of mass of the thin homogeneous wire bent into the shape shown.

PROBLEM 3.1.9

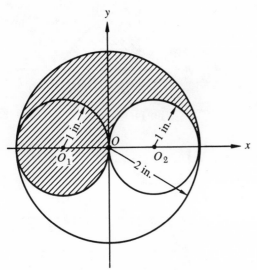

Locate the centroid of the shaded area shown. The outer circle has a radius of 2 in. The diameters of the two inner circles are 2 in. each.

PROBLEM 3.1.10

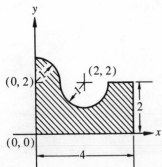

Locate the centroid of the shaded area shown. What is the volume generated by rotating the shaded area about the x-axis through 2π radians?

Applications in plane statics

Locate the center of mass of the right rectangular pyramid shown. The density ρ is given by the relation $\rho = \rho_0 + kx^2$, where ρ_0 and k are constants and x is the height from the base.

PROBLEM 3.1.11

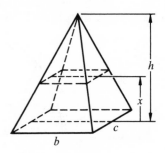

Locate the centroid of the shaded area shown.

PROBLEM 3.1.12

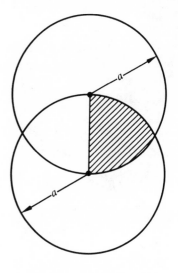

Locate the centroid of the volume generated by revolving the right triangle of altitude a about its base b through an angle θ.

PROBLEM 3.1.13

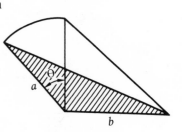

PROBLEM 3.1.14   Determine the centroid of the solid spherical wedge shown.

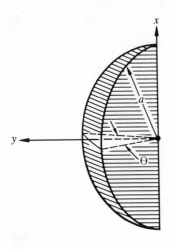

PROBLEM 3.1.15   Locate the center of mass of the body consisting of a thin half-cylindrical shell of area density 4.2 lb/ft² closed at one end by a thin semicircular sheet of area density 6.8 lb/ft².

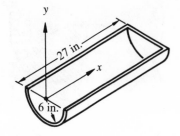

Section 3.2   Friction

SAMPLE PROBLEM   The chain shown weighs δ lb/ft and has a length of $\pi r/2$ ft. The coefficient of static friction, μ, between the chain and its semicircular support, is sufficiently large to prevent slipping in the absence of forces other than weight and reaction of the support. What horizontal force **P** must be applied at the upper end of the chain to start it moving?

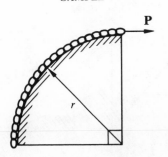

Applications in plane statics

Solution

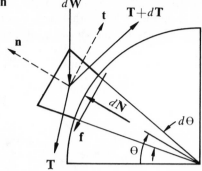

$$\Sigma\mathbf{F} = 0: \qquad \mathbf{T} + d\mathbf{T} - \mathbf{T} + d\mathbf{N} + \mathbf{f} + d\mathbf{W} = 0$$

where $\qquad |d\mathbf{W}| = \delta r\, d\theta \qquad |\mathbf{f}| = \mu|d\mathbf{N}|$

Taking tangential and normal components, we get

$$dT\cos(\tfrac{1}{2}\, d\theta) - \mu\, dN - \delta r\, d\theta \cos\theta = 0$$

$$-\, dT\sin(\tfrac{1}{2}\, d\theta) + dN - \delta r\, d\theta \sin\theta = 0$$

However, $\qquad \cos(\tfrac{1}{2}\, d\theta) = 1 \qquad \sin(\tfrac{1}{2}\, d\theta) = \tfrac{1}{2}\, d\theta$

so that $\qquad dT - \delta r\cos\theta\, d\theta = \mu\, dN$

$$(\delta r\sin\theta + T)\, d\theta = dN$$

Eliminating dN and dividing by $d\theta$ now yields the linear first-order differential equation

$$\frac{dT}{d\theta} - \mu T = \delta r(\mu\sin\theta + \cos\theta)$$

whose solution is

$$T = C\exp(\mu\theta) + \frac{\delta r}{1 + \mu^2}\left[(1 - \mu^2)\sin\theta - 2\mu\cos\theta\right]$$

To compute the constant of integration C, we use initial condition

$$\theta = 0: \qquad T = 0$$

so that $\qquad C = \dfrac{2\,\delta r\mu}{1 + \mu^2}$

But at $\theta = \dfrac{\pi}{2}$, $T = P$. Hence

$$P = \frac{\delta r}{1 + \mu^2}\left[2\mu\exp\left(\frac{\mu\pi}{2}\right) + 1 - \mu^2\right]$$

Friction 37

PROBLEM 3.2.1

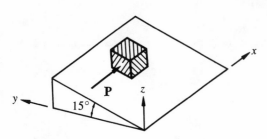

Determine the maximum force **P** in the direction of the *x*-axis that can be applied to the 50-lb crate shown without producing slipping. The static coefficient of friction between the crate and the incline is 0.4.

PROBLEM 3.2.2 A homogeneous cylinder of weight *W* is held in equilibrium by the horizontal force **P** as shown. For a given θ, find the minimum coefficient of friction required to prevent slipping.

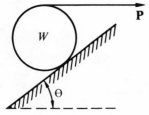

PROBLEM 3.2.3

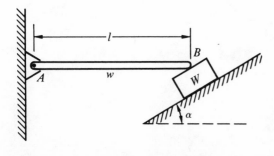

A uniform bar of weight *w* and length *l* is pinned in a frictionless joint at end *A*. The bar is horizontal, and its end *B* rests on a block of weight *W*. The block rests on a plane inclined at angle α to the horizontal. If the friction between the bar and block is negligible, show that the minimum coefficient of friction between the block and plane required to maintain the system in equilibrium is

$$\mu = \frac{\sin 2\alpha}{2 \cos^2 \alpha + (w/W)}$$

Applications in plane statics

A homogeneous thin-walled angle bar is supported by the edge of a horizontal table at a point located at distance x from apex A. If the static coefficient of friction between the bar and the table is 0.1, determine the maximum distance x for equilibrium.

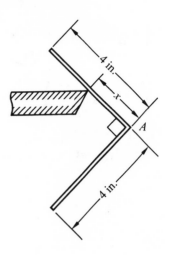

A rod of negligible weight is placed on a smooth roller at B and against a rough vertical wall at A as shown. The coefficient of static friction between rod and wall is 0.25. A sleeve of weight W is pinned to the bar at point C. Is the coefficient of friction sufficiently large to prevent motion?

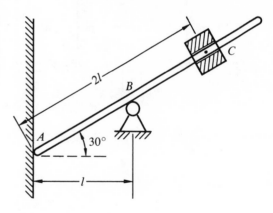

A homogeneous semicircular cylinder of radius R and weight W rests on a horizontal plane such that its edge makes an angle α with the horizontal when it is subjected to a horizontal force $\mathbf{P}$ acting at right angles to the cylinder axis in the vertical plane containing the center of mass C. Determine the magnitude of the force $\mathbf{P}$ and the angle α when motion is impending. The coefficient of friction between the cylinder and the horizontal plane is μ.

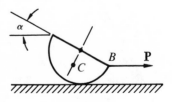

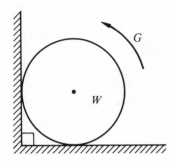

PROBLEM 3.2.7 What is the couple G if motion is impending for the wheel of weight W and radius r shown? The coefficient of friction for all surfaces is μ.

PROBLEM 3.2.8

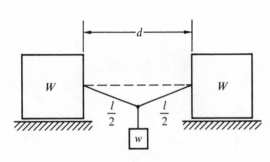

Two blocks of equal weights W can slide on the horizontal surface shown. A light string of length l is suspended between the blocks and carries a weight w at its mid-point. What is the maximum value of d so that sliding does not take place? The coefficient of friction between the blocks and the surface is μ.

PROBLEM 3.2.9

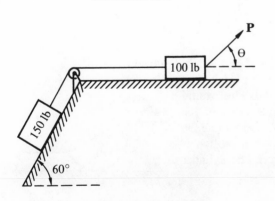

What is the minimum value of the force **P** and the corresponding value of angle θ when motion to the right is impending? The coefficient of friction for all surfaces is 0.2. Neglect the mass and friction of the pulley.

40   *Applications in plane statics*

What horizontal force **P** acting on the wedges B and C is necessary to just raise the load of 20 tons applied at the center of support A? The coefficient of friction is 0.25 between the wedges and the ground and 0.2 between the wedges and the support. Neglect the weights of the wedges and of the support.

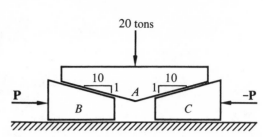

Section 3.3   Thin beams

Determine the variations of shear S and moment M along the thin beam shown. Draw the shear and moment diagrams.

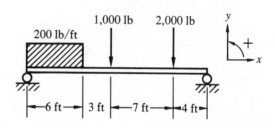

Solution

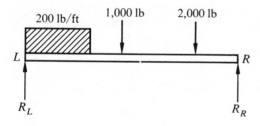

First find the reactions at the ends:

$$\Sigma M_L = 0 = -1,200(3) - 1,000(9) - 2,000(16) + 20R_R$$
$$R_R = 2,230 \text{ lb}$$

$$\Sigma M_R = 0 = -20R_L + 1,200(17) + 1,000(11) + 2,000(4)$$
$$R_L = 1,970 \text{ lb}$$

Thin beams   41

Now examine the beam in the interval $0 < x < 6$:

$$\Sigma F_y = 0 = 1{,}970 - 200x - S$$

Therefore, $\qquad S = 1{,}970 - 200x \text{ lb}$

$$\Sigma M_0 = 0 = -1.970x + 200\left(\frac{x}{2}\right) + M$$

Therefore, $\qquad M = 1{,}970x - 100x^2 \text{ lb-ft}$

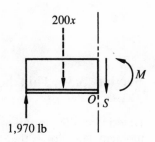

Similarly, for $6 < x < 9$:

$$S = 1{,}970 - 1{,}200 = 770 \text{ lb}$$

$$M = 1.970x - 1{,}200(x - 3) = 770x + 3{,}600 \text{ lb-ft}$$

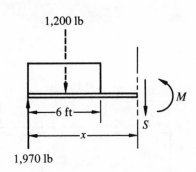

In the same way we consider the intervals $9 < x < 16$ and $16 < x < 20$, drawing free-body diagrams for each case.

For $9 < x < 16$:
$$S = -230 \text{ lb} \quad \text{and} \quad M = -230x + 12{,}600 \text{ lb-ft}$$

For $16 < x < 20$:
$$S = -2{,}230 \text{ lb} \quad \text{and} \quad M = -2{,}230x + 44{,}600 \text{ lb-ft}$$

Applications in plane statics

Now the shear and moment diagrams can be drawn:

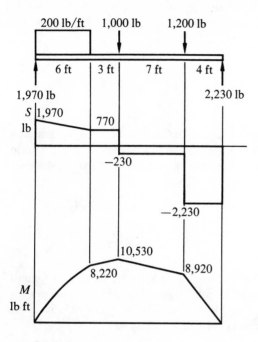

Determine the shear and moment equations for the beam shown. Draw the shear and moment diagrams.

PROBLEM 3.3.1

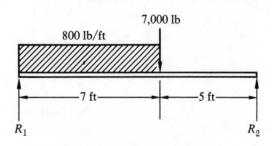

Plot the shear diagram and find the maximum bending moment for the beam shown.

PROBLEM 3.3.2

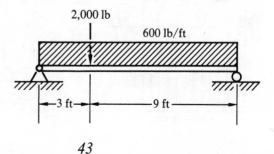

Thin beams

PROBLEM 3.3.3

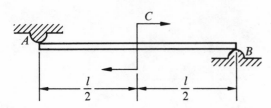

Draw the shear and moment diagrams for the beam loaded at its center by the couple C. Is the bending moment defined at the mid-point? Explain.

PROBLEM 3.3.4

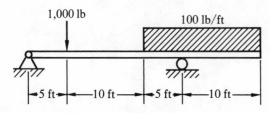

Draw the shear and moment diagrams for the beam shown. Determine the magnitude and location of the maximum vertical shear.

PROBLEM 3.3.5

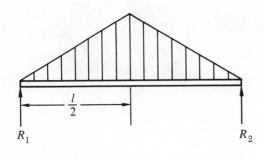

Show that the maximum bending moment for a thin beam loaded as shown is $M = \frac{1}{6}Wl$, where W is the total load on the beam and l is the span.

Section 3.4 Flexible cables

SAMPLE PROBLEM

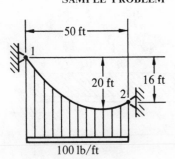

The light flexible cable shown supports a load of 100 lb/ft uniformly distributed in the horizontal direction. Find the maximum tension $T_{\max}$ and the minimum tension $T_{\min}$.

Solution

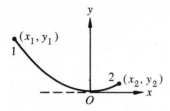

Using the coordinate system with origin at the lowest point, we have

$$x_2 - x_1 = 50 \text{ ft} \qquad y_1 = 20 \text{ ft} \qquad y_2 = 4 \text{ ft}$$

The equation of the cable is

$$y = \frac{w_0 x^2}{2H}$$

where w_0 = load per unit horizontal distance

H = horizontal component of tension = const

Writing this equation at

Point 1: $\qquad\qquad 20 = \dfrac{100 x_1{}^2}{2H}$

Point 2: $\qquad\qquad 4 = \dfrac{100 x_2{}^2}{2H}$

so that $\qquad\qquad x_1{}^2 = 5 x_2{}^2 \qquad\qquad$ (1)

But $\qquad\qquad x_2 = x_1 + 50$

so that (1) becomes

$$x_1{}^2 + 125 x_1 + 3{,}125 = 0 \qquad\qquad (2)$$

whence $\qquad x_1 = -34.5 \text{ ft} \qquad x_1 = -90.4 \text{ ft}$

The second root is discarded since $|x_1| < 50$ ft.
We can now evaluate H at point 1; namely,

$$H = \frac{100(34.5)^2}{2(20)} = 2{,}970 \text{ lb}$$

Tension is maximum at point 1 and is given by

$$T = T_{\max} = (H^2 + w_0{}^2 x_1{}^2)^{1/2} = 4{,}560 \text{ lb}$$

Tension is minimum at the lowest point and is

$$T = T_{\min} = H = 2{,}980 \text{ lb}$$

Flexible cables $\qquad\qquad\qquad\qquad\qquad\qquad\qquad\qquad$ 45

PROBLEM 3.4.1

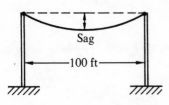

A flexible cable is stretched between two poles from points at the same elevation. The span between the poles is 100 ft. Find the minimum sag in the cable if the tension is not to exceed 150 lb. Twenty feet of the cable weighs 1 lb. Consider two cases:

(a) The weight of the cable is distributed uniformly in the horizontal direction;

(b) The weight of the cable is distributed uniformly along its length.

PROBLEM 3.4.2

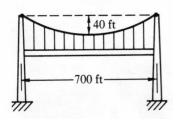

A cable of a suspension bridge carries a load of 1,000 lb per horizontal foot. The span is 700 ft and the sag is 40 ft. The weight of the cable is neglected. Determine the maximum tension in the cable.

PROBLEM 3.4.3

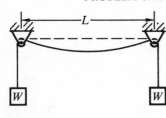

A flexible cable is supported by two small frictionless pulleys and carries at its ends two equal weights $W = 500$ lb as shown. The span $L = 100$ ft and the pulleys are at the same height. Find the deflection of the cable at mid-span:

(a) Assuming that the weight of the cable is uniformly distributed with respect to the horizontal span and is 2 lb/ft;

(b) Assuming that the cable is uniform and weighs 2 lb/ft of its length.

PROBLEM 3.4.4

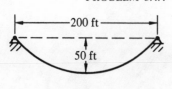

A flexible cable weighs 0.5 lb/ft of length. It is stretched between two supports at the same level 200 ft apart. The sag is 50 ft. Find the length of the cable and the maximum tension in the cable.

Applications in plane statics

Block *B* shown in the figure weighs 100 lb. The coefficient of friction between each of the blocks and the inclined planes is 0.20. The coefficient of friction between the light cable connecting the blocks and the quarter circle support *C* is $1/\pi$. Determine the maximum weight of block *A* so that the system will remain in equilibrium.

PROBLEM 3.4.5

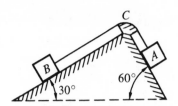

A light rope is wrapped three full turns around a capstan in order to help support a load of 1,000 lb. If the coefficient of friction $\mu = 0.25$, find the force **F** required to hold the load at rest.

PROBLEM 3.4.6

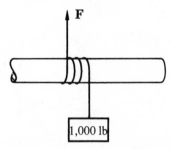

The light rope of a boy's swing is wrapped halfway around the limb of a tree. If the boy weighs 100 lb, what pull must he exert on the free end of the rope to hold himself in equilibrium? The coefficient of friction between the limb and rope is $\mu = 0.4$.

PROBLEM 3.4.7

Limb of tree

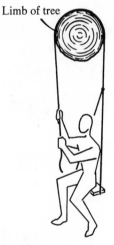

Two identical rotating drums with a diameter of 30 in. are connected by a continuous light belt as shown. The tension in the tight side of the belt is 200 lb. If the coefficient of friction is 0.25, determine the tension in the slack side of the belt when slipping is impending.

PROBLEM 3.4.8

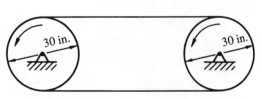

Flexible cables

The tension at one end of a belt, which is wrapped around three fixed drums as shown, is 15 lb. Determine the range of values of the tension T for equilibrium, if the coefficient of friction between the belt and each drum is $\mu = 1/\pi$.

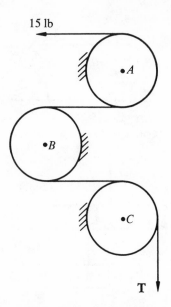

15 lb

Section 3.5   Frames

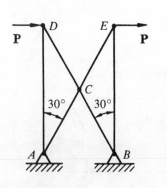

SAMPLE PROBLEM   The simple frame shown is made up of six members which are pinned smoothly at joints A, B, C, D, and E. Two equal horizontal forces of magnitude P are applied at joints D and E. Utilizing the method of joints, determine the force in each member of the frame in terms of P. Indicate whether the member is in tension (T) or compression (C).

Applications in plane statics

Solution

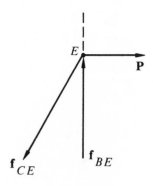

$$\Sigma \mathbf{F} = 0: \qquad \mathbf{f}_{CE} + \mathbf{f}_{BE} + \mathbf{P} = 0$$
$$f_{CE} = 2P \qquad (T)$$
$$f_{BE} = \sqrt{3}P \qquad (C)$$

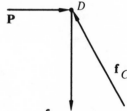

$$\Sigma \mathbf{F} = 0: \qquad \mathbf{f}_{AD} + \mathbf{f}_{CD} + \mathbf{P} = 0$$
$$f_{CD} = 2P \qquad (C)$$
$$f_{AD} = \sqrt{3}P \qquad (T)$$

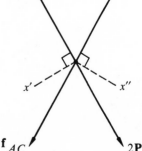

$$\Sigma F_{x'} = 0: \qquad f_{AC} = 2P \qquad (T)$$
$$\Sigma F_{x''} = 0: \qquad f_{BC} = 2P \qquad (C)$$

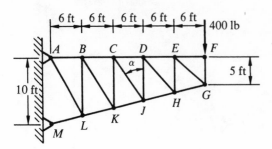

The simple frame shown consists of 20 members smoothly hinged at the joints. A vertical load of 400 lb is applied at joint F. Calculate the force in member CJ using a single equation of equilibrium.

Solution

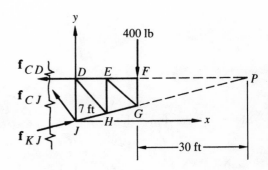

The statement of the problem implies the use of the method of sections. A vertical section is made through member CJ. The lines of action of forces $\mathbf{f}_{CD}$ and $\mathbf{f}_{KJ}$ intersect at point P. A moment sum about point P involves the applied load and force $\mathbf{f}_{CJ}$ only.

Consider the xy-coordinate system shown:

$$\mathbf{f}_{CJ} = \frac{f_{CJ}}{\sqrt{6^2 + 7^2}}(-6\mathbf{i} + 7\mathbf{j})$$

$$\Sigma\,\mathbf{M}_P = 0: \qquad \vec{PJ} \times \mathbf{f}_{CJ} + (-30\mathbf{i}) \times (-400\mathbf{j}) = 0$$

$$f_{CJ} = 329 \text{ lb} \qquad (T)$$

Applications in plane statics

The hoisting mechanism shown is used to support a 6,000-lb load by means of a pulley system. The hoisting cable is secured to the fixed drum at H. The pulleys at D and G are of equal radius. Determine the x- and y-components of all forces acting on member GE. Neglect the weight of the hoisting mechanism and friction.

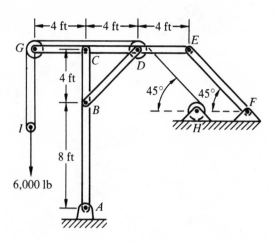

Solution

Forces in (a), (b), and (c) are obtained by successively applying $\Sigma F = 0$. Since EF is a two-force member inclined at 45°, $E_x = E_y$. From (d),

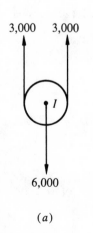

(a)

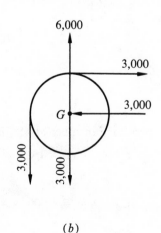

(b)

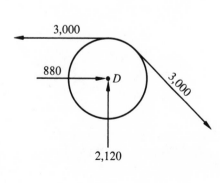

(c)

Frames

51

$$\Sigma \mathbf{M}_A = 0: \quad (4)(6,000) + (12)(880) + 12E_x$$
$$+ 8E_x - (12)(3,000) - (4)(2,120) = 0$$
$$E_x = E_y = 496 \text{ lb}$$

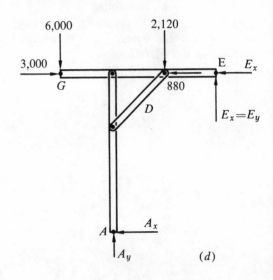

(d)

From (e),

$$\Sigma \mathbf{M}_C = 0: \quad (4)(6,000) - 4D_y - (4)(2,120) + (8)(496) = 0$$

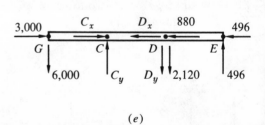

(e)

Since BD is a two-force member at 45°, $D_x = D_y = 4,870$ lb.

$$\Sigma F_x = 0: \quad C_x + 3,000 - 4,870 - 880 - 496 = 0$$
$$C_x = 3,250 \text{ lb}$$
$$\Sigma F_y = 0: \quad C_y + 496 - 6,000 - 4,870 - 2,120 = 0$$
$$C_y = 12,500 \text{ lb}$$

Applications in plane statics

The two light members *AB* and *BC*, pinned smoothly at the ends, form a single frame. A horizontal force of 100 lb is applied at joint *B*. Find the forces in members *AB* and *BC*.

PROBLEM 3.5.1

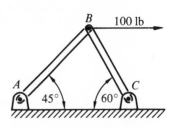

A simple frame supports a 5,000-lb load by the pulley system shown. Find the forces in the members of the frame. Indicate whether a member is in tension or compression. Neglect weights of pulleys.

PROBLEM 3.5.2

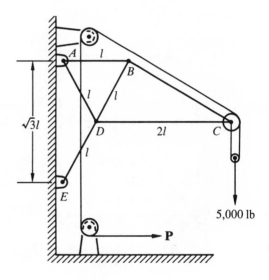

The simple frame shown is loaded at *C* by a 4-ton weight. A horizontal force of 2 tons is applied at *D*. Joint *A* is pinned to a fixed support. Joint *E* is pinned to a support on rollers. Find the forces in the members.

PROBLEM 3.5.3

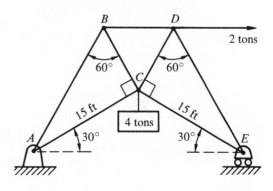

Frames   53

PROBLEM 3.5.4

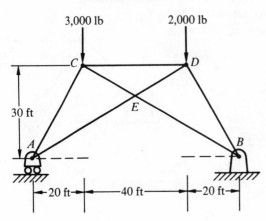

3,000 lb   2,000 lb

C   D

E

30 ft

A   B

←20 ft→←——40 ft——→←20 ft→

The two basic triangular frames *ACD* and *BCD* are pinned together at *C* and *D* to form a simple truss. Joint *A* is pinned to a rolling support and joint *B* to a fixed support. The truss is subjected to vertical loads of 3,000 lb at *C* and 2,000 lb at *D*. Find the reactions at *A* and *B* and the forces in all members of the truss.

PROBLEM 3.5.5

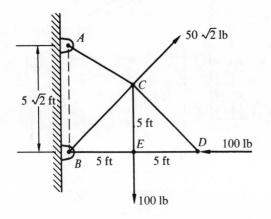

A

$5\sqrt{2}$ ft

$50\sqrt{2}$ lb

C

5 ft

E   D   100 lb

B   5 ft   5 ft

100 lb

The simple truss shown is subjected to loads at *C*, *D*, and *E* as shown. Find the reactions at the supports *A* and *B* and the forces in the members of the truss.

PROBLEM 3.5.6

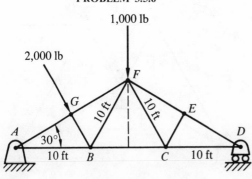

1,000 lb

2,000 lb

G   F   E

10 ft   10 ft

A   30°   D

10 ft   B   C   10 ft

A symmetric simple roof truss fixed at *A* and resting on rollers at *D* is subjected to the loads shown. Determine the reactions at *A* and *D*. Find the forces in members *FC* and *CE*.

54

The simple truss shown is subjected to two vertical loads. Determine the forces in members BF, FC, and CE.

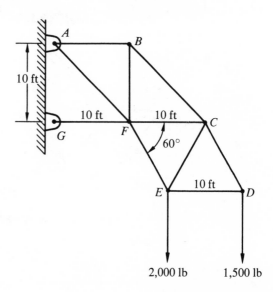

The simple railroad truss shown is subjected to vertical loads at C and F and to a horizontal load at H. Joint A is pinned to a fixed support and joint E is pinned to a roller. Determine the reactions at A and E and the force in member GB.

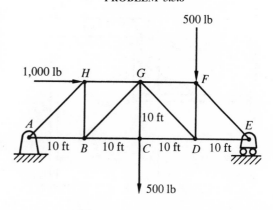

Frames

55

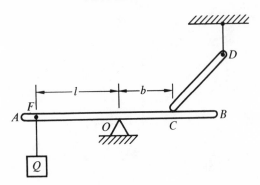

The uniform rod AB of weight w is pivoted at its center O. The second uniform rod CD of weight W rests on AB as shown, being supported at the other end by a vertical cable attached to a fixed support. The weight Q is hung from AB by a wire at F, a distance l from O. Find the expression for $b = \overline{OC}$ in terms of w, $l = \overline{OF}$, W, and Q, such that rod AB is in equilibrium in the horizontal position. Neglect friction.

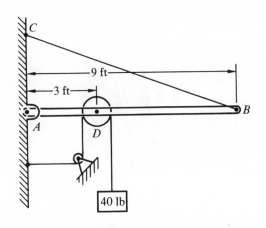

The uniform beam supports a 40-lb weight by means of the pulley mechanism shown. The beam is pinned to a fixed support A and is held by light cable BC. The beam weighs 100 lb and the pulley at D weighs 50 lb. Find the force exerted by the pulley axle on the beam and the total reaction at A. Neglect friction in the pulleys.

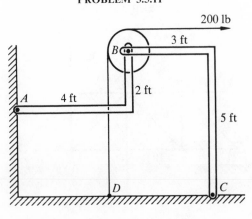

The two L-shaped members are pinned to fixed supports at A and C, respectively, and to each other at B, where they support a pulley. A cable attached at D passes over the pulley and is subjected to a 200-lb horizontal force. Find the force acting on member AB at A. Neglect the weights of members AB, BC, the pulley, and the cable, as well as friction in pins and at the pulley.

Applications in plane statics

A smooth ball of radius R and weight Q is supported by two inclined uniform bars OA and OB, each of length l and weight W. The bars are hinged smoothly at support O and rest at A and B against smooth vertical walls as shown. Use the principle of virtual work to determine the reactions at A and B.

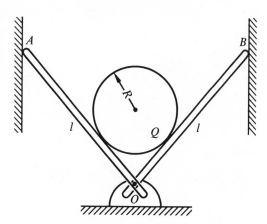

The pinned structure shown is made up of light members and is subjected to a vertical load of 100 lb at joint B. Find the forces exerted on members AE and BD at pin C.

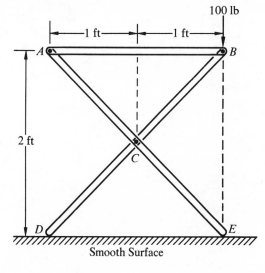

Smooth Surface

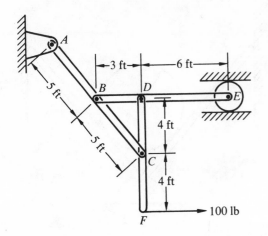

The pinned structure shown consists of three light bars pinned to one another at B, C, and D. Bar AC is pinned to a fixed support at A. Horizontal bar BE is supported by a light guided roller at E. A horizontal 100-lb force is applied to vertical bar DF. Determine the forces exerted on the pins at A, B, C, and E. Neglect friction.

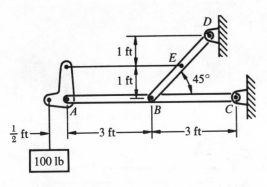

The structure shown consists of members AC and BC pinned to each other at B. A bell crank is pinned to horizontal member AC at A. A 100-lb weight hangs from one arm of the bell crank, and the other arm is tied to member BD by a cable as shown. Determine the force acting on the pin at B. Neglect the weight of all components of the structure, as well as friction at the pins.

Applications in plane statics

PLANE KINEMATICS

Section 4.1   Kinematics of a particle

SAMPLE PROBLEM

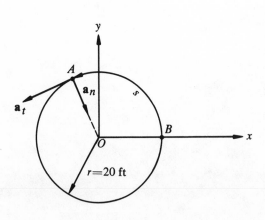

Particle *A* moves on a circular path of radius 20 ft such that its distance from initial point *B* is given by $s = 6t^3 - 4t$, where *s* is in ft and *t* is in sec. Find the tangential and normal components of acceleration of the particle at $t = 2$ sec.

60

CHAPTER 4

Solution

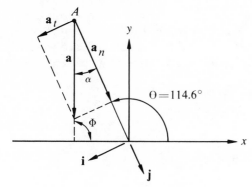

$$\mathbf{v} = \frac{ds}{dt}\,\mathbf{i}: \qquad v = \frac{d}{dt}\,(6t^3 - 4t) = 18t^2 - 4 \qquad (1)$$

$$a_t = \frac{dv}{dt}: \qquad a_t = \frac{d}{dt}\,(18t^2 - 4) = 36t \qquad (2)$$

Hence for $t = 2$ in (1) and (2), we have

$$v = 18(2)^2 - 4 = 68 \text{ ft/sec}$$

$$a_t = 36(2) = 72 \text{ ft/sec}^2$$

$$a_n = v^2/r: \qquad a_n = (68)^2/20 = 231 \text{ ft/sec}^2$$

$$a = \sqrt{a_n{}^2 + a_t{}^2}: \qquad a = \sqrt{(231)^2 + (72)^2} = 242 \text{ ft/sec}^2$$

To find the inclination Φ of the resultant acceleration, we have

$$s = 6t^3 - 4t: \qquad s = 6(2)^3 - 4(2) = 40 \text{ ft}$$

$$\theta = s/r: \qquad \theta = 40/20 = 2 \text{ radians} = 114.6°$$

From the figure above, we have

$$\tan \alpha = a_t/a_n: \qquad \tan \alpha = 72/231 \quad \text{or} \quad \alpha = 17.3°$$

$$\Phi = \theta - \alpha = 114.6° - 17.3° = 97.3°$$

PROBLEM 4.1.1 The distance traveled by a particle moving in a straight line is given by s. Its acceleration is

$$\mathbf{a} = \mathbf{a}_0 \sin \frac{2\pi s}{L} \qquad \mathbf{a}_0 = \text{const}$$

If the initial velocity $\mathbf{v}(0) = \mathbf{v}_0$, find the velocity when **(a)** $s = L/4$; **(b)** $s = L/2$.

PROBLEM 4.1.2

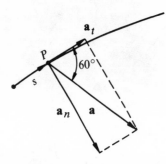

A particle P moves along a plane curve such that the distance traveled is given by $s = b(e^{kt} - 1)$ with b and k constants. The acceleration $\mathbf{a}$ is always inclined to its tangential component at an angle of 60°. Find the velocity and acceleration of particle P and the radius of curvature of its path in terms of the distance s.

PROBLEM 4.1.3

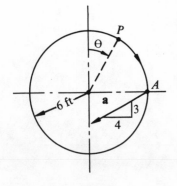

A particle P moves clockwise on a circular path of 6-ft radius. When it is at the point A, it has an acceleration of 60 ft/sec² in the direction shown. At this point find
(a) The component of the acceleration due to a change in direction of the velocity;
(b) The component due to a change in magnitude of the velocity;
(c) The values of $\dot{\theta}$ and $\ddot{\theta}$.

62

The rod shown in the figure rotates in a horizontal plane
with a constant angular speed $\dot{\theta} = 10$ radians/sec. The
sliding block moves outward on the rod at a rate of 10 in./sec.
Displacement $r = 0$ when $\theta = 0$. Find the acceleration of
the block when $r = 5$ in.

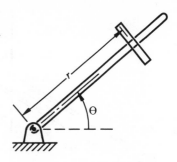

A particle starts from rest and moves in a
straight line with an acceleration as shown
in the graph. Draw the corresponding
velocity-time curve and displacement-time
curve. What are the velocity and the displacement at $t = 5$ sec?

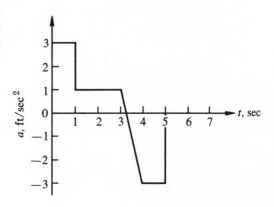

A particle moves in a plane such that the normal and
tangential components of its acceleration are constant.
Derive the equation of the path of the particle.

Derive expressions for the displacement,
velocity, and acceleration of the slider P for
any position of the crank AB rotating at
constant angular speed ω radians/sec. Show
that the acceleration of P is given approximately by

$$\mathbf{a} = r\omega^2 \left(\cos \theta + \frac{r}{l} \cos 2\theta \right) \mathbf{i}$$

provided that $r^2/l^2 \ll 1$.

Kinematics of a particle   63

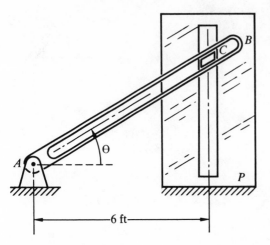

Block *C* moves vertically in the slot of plate *P* and is also constrained to move in the slot of rotating arm *AB*. Find the velocity and acceleration of block *C* when $\theta = 30°$, $\dot{\theta} = 6$ radians/sec, and $\ddot{\theta} = 3$ radians/sec^2.

—6 ft—

PROBLEM 4.1.9 A particle *P* moves on a plane path such that its tangential acceleration is always zero. Show that $r^2\dot{\Phi} = $ constant.

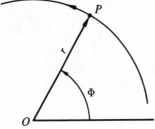

PROBLEM 4.1.10 At the bottom of a circular loop a particle has a normal component of acceleration $a_n = 100$ ft/sec^2 and a speed $v = 400$ ft/sec. Find the radius *R* of the loop.

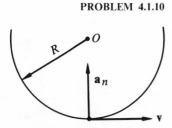

PROBLEM 4.1.11 The motion of a particle on a circle of radius *r* is given by $x = r \sin \omega t$, $y = r \cos \omega t$, where $\omega = $ constant. Find the velocity and the acceleration at time *t* in terms of rectangular coordinates *x,y* and polar coordinates *r,θ*, respectively.

64   *Plane kinematics*

Section 4.2 Motion of a rigid body parallel to a fixed plane

A four-link mechanism consists of two cranks AB and DC connected by link BC. Ends A and D are pinned to fixed supports. The mechanism occupies the position shown in the figure when the angular velocity of AB is $\omega_{AB} = 11$ radians/sec counterclockwise. Locate the instantaneous center of BC, and determine the velocity of C, the angular velocity of CD, and the velocity of any point M on BC.

SAMPLE PROBLEM

Solution

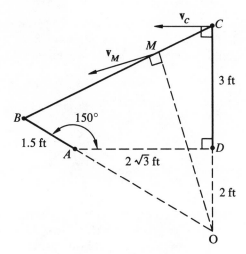

Points B and C are constrained to move on circles about A and D, respectively; hence, the instantaneous center O is the intersection of the extensions of AB and CD.

$$\overline{DO} = \overline{AD} \tan 30° = 3.464 \times .577 = 2 \text{ ft}$$

$$\overline{AO} = \frac{\overline{AD}}{\cos 30°} = \frac{3.464}{.866} = 4 \text{ ft}$$

$v_B = \overline{AB}\omega_{AB} = \overline{BO}\omega_{BC}$:

$$1.5 \times 11 = 5.5\omega_{BC} \qquad \omega_{BC} = 3 \text{ radians/sec}$$

Motion of a rigid body parallel to a fixed plane

$$v_C = \overline{CO}\omega_{BC} = \overline{CD}\omega_{CD}:$$

$$v_C = (3 + 2) \times 3 = 15 \text{ ft/sec}$$

$$15 = 3\omega_{CD} \qquad \omega_{CD} = 5 \text{ radians/sec}$$

The velocity of any other point M is found by scaling the distance $\overline{MO}$ and applying $v_M = \overline{MO}\omega_{BC}$. The direction of $\mathbf{v}_M$ is perpendicular to $\overline{MO}$ as shown.

PROBLEM 4.2.1   A wheel rolls to the right without slipping with angular speed ω. Show that the velocity of the center O is given by $r\omega\mathbf{i}$. Determine the velocity of points A and B at the instant shown.

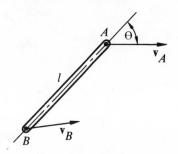

PROBLEM 4.2.2   A rigid bar moves in a plane as shown in the figure. Find an expression for the angular velocity of the bar in terms of $\mathbf{v}_A$, $\mathbf{v}_B$, θ, and l.

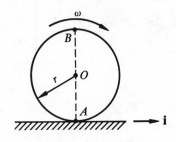

PROBLEM 4.2.3   Triangular plate ABC is constrained to move in the vertical plane. Corner A is pinned to a slider which moves in a vertical groove; corner B is similarly constrained to move along a horizontal groove. At the instant shown B has a velocity of 4 ft/sec to the right. Calculate the velocity of corner C and the angular velocity of the plate.

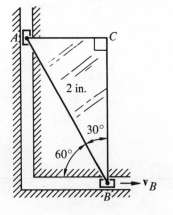

A wheel rotates about the fixed axis at O with a constant angular speed $\omega = 10$ rpm. Link AB is 10 in. and connects point A on the wheel to end B of crank CB which rotates with point C fixed. Find the angular velocity of link AB for the position shown.

PROBLEM 4.2.4

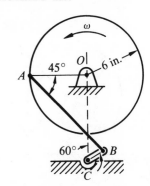

Cylinder C rolls without slipping on block B. Determine the angular velocity of the cylinder, if the block has a velocity $\mathbf{v}_B = 4$ ft/sec to the right, and the center O of the roller has a velocity $\mathbf{v}_0 = 4$ ft/sec to the left. The radius of the roller is 6 in.

PROBLEM 4.2.5

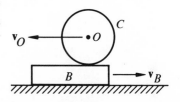

Blocks A and B move in parallel directions as shown causing the wheel in contact with them to move. If there is no slipping between the wheel and the blocks, calculate the velocity of center O of the wheel and find the instantaneous center of the wheel.

PROBLEM 4.2.6

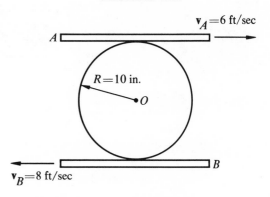

The outer track shown is stationary. The crank $O_1 O_2$ has end O_1 pinned to a fixed support and turns at an angular speed ω. Roller R_1 with center at O_1 is in contact with roller R_2 with center at O_2. If there is no slipping between R_1 and R_2, and R_2 and the track, find the angular velocity of roller R_1 and the instantaneous center of R_2.

PROBLEM 4.2.7

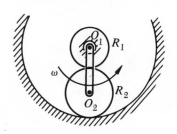

PROBLEM 4.2.8

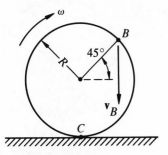

A cylinder of radius $R = 2$ ft, in contact with a horizontal plane, is in planar motion. At a given instant, its angular speed $\omega = 20$ radians/sec and point B has a velocity of $\mathbf{v}_B$ vertically downward. Find the velocity of the point of contact C.

METHODS
OF PLANE DYNAMICS

Section 5.1   Motion of a particle

SAMPLE PROBLEM   A force $\mathbf{F}(t)$ acts on a particle of mass m lying on a smooth table and attached to a light bar of length L whose other end pivots about fixed point O. The force acts in the horizontal plane and is always perpendicular to the bar. If the particle is initially at rest in position $\theta = \theta_0$ and the force has magnitude

$$F(t) = A \sin \Omega t$$

where A and Ω are constant, determine the displacement angle θ and the force exerted by the bar on the particle as a function of time.

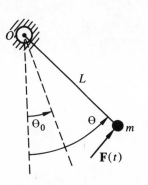

Solution

Using normal and tangential components:

$$\mathbf{F} = m\mathbf{a}: \qquad F_t = m\frac{dv}{dt}: \qquad A \sin \Omega t = mL\ddot{\theta}$$

$$\dot{\theta} - (0) = \frac{A}{mL\Omega}(1 - \cos \Omega t)$$

$$\theta - \theta_0 = \frac{A}{mL\Omega}\left(t - \frac{\sin \Omega t}{\Omega}\right)$$

$$F_n = \frac{mv^2}{\rho}: \qquad F_n = \frac{m}{L}L^2\dot{\theta}^2 = \frac{A^2}{mL\Omega^2}(1 - \cos \Omega t)^2$$

CHAPTER 5

A bead of weight $W = \frac{1}{2}$ lb slides down a smooth stationary wire shaped in the form of parabola $y = x^2$. The bead starts from rest at point $(3,9)$.

PROBLEM 5.1.1

(a) Find the velocity of the bead at the lowest point $(0,0)$.
(b) Find the force exerted on the bead by the wire at the lowest point.

A small mass of weight W, starting from rest, moves down a frictionless slide and enters a frictionless circular loop of radius r, as shown. Find the minimum height h from which the mass must start in order that it remain in contact with the loop.

PROBLEM 5.1.2

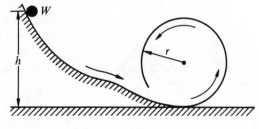

PROBLEM 5.1.3 Find the accelerations of the weights and the tensions in the inextensible cords of the frictionless pulley system shown. Neglect the masses of the pulleys and cords, and treat the weights as particles.

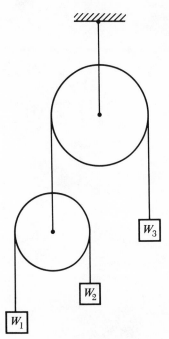

PROBLEM 5.1.4 A bob of mass $m = 25$ g is attached to one end of a light cord of length $L = 1$ m whose other end is fixed. The bob is set into circular motion in the horizontal plane. The radius of the circular path is R, and the horizontal projection of the cord has a constant angular speed $\omega = 25$ radians/sec.

(a) Determine radius R and tension T in the cord.

(b) Determine the angular momentum of the bob with respect to the center of the circular path.

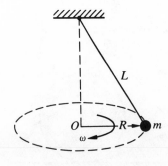

Methods of plane dynamics

A small body of mass m is attached to a weightless string and moves in a circular path on a smooth horizontal table. Initially, the radius of the path is 24 in. and has an angular velocity of 1 radian/sec clockwise. The string is continuously shortened by pulling it through a hole in the support as shown. If the final radius of the path is 8 in., what is the angular velocity of the string? What is the relation between the initial and final tension in the string?

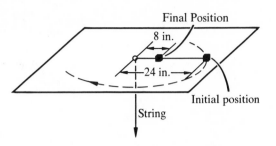

Final Position

8 in.

24 in.

Initial position

String

A linear spring with constant $k = 120$ lb/in. supports a block of weight $W = 200$ lb as shown. The block is not fastened to the spring and the guide is frictionless. A force F which gradually increases to a maximum value of 400 lb is applied to the block.
(a) What is the increase in the spring deflection due to the action of force F?
(b) If the force F is suddenly removed, what is the maximum height the 200-lb block will attain above the equilibrium position of the spring under the action of W and F?

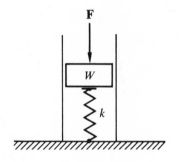

F

W

k

A water tank on top of a 100-ft tower can be filled by pumping in water either (a) at the top of the tank, or (b) at the bottom of the tank. Which method is more efficient, i.e., requires less work? Explain.

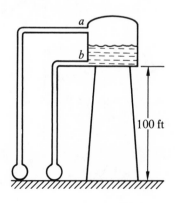

a

b

100 ft

Motion of a particle

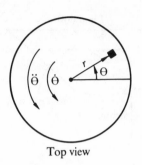

Top view

PROBLEM 5.1.8 A small block of weight W is placed on the horizontal surface of a circular disk at a distance r from the fixed center of the disk. The coefficient of friction between the block and the disk is μ. If the disk starts to move from rest with a constant angular acceleration $\ddot{\theta}$, find the value of the angular speed $\dot{\theta}$ at which the block begins to slip.

PROBLEM 5.1.9 A particle P of mass m rests at the top of a smooth parabolic surface whose equation is $x^2 = -4by$ where the y-axis is vertical and b is a constant. The particle is given a small displacement, causing it to slide down the surface.
(a) Find the force $\mathbf{N}$ exerted by the surface on particle P as a function of its vertical displacement.
(b) Does the particle leave the surface? Explain.

PROBLEM 5.1.10

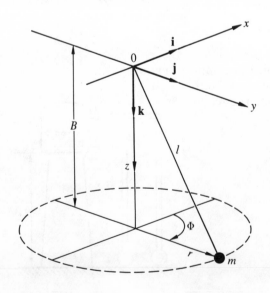

The pendulum shown has a bob of mass m suspended at the end of a weightless cord of length l. The bob is moving on a circular path in the horizontal plane a distance B below the point of suspension O. The rate of change of the angle ϕ in the plane of motion is $\omega = $ constant.
(a) What is the linear momentum of the particle in terms of components in the directions of the stationary $\mathbf{i}$, $\mathbf{j}$, and $\mathbf{k}$ unit vectors?
(b) What is the angular momentum of the particle with respect to point O in terms of $\mathbf{i}$, $\mathbf{j}$, and $\mathbf{k}$ components?
(c) What causes the change in linear momentum?
(d) What causes the change in angular momentum?

74

The cord of the pendulum described in Prob. 5.1.10 is suddenly cut. Describe the subsequent motion of the bob.

PROBLEM 5.1.11

The coefficient of friction between block B and inclined plane S is μ. Coefficient μ is less than $\tan \phi$, where ϕ is the angle of inclination. The block is projected up the plane with a velocity v_0, and returns to its starting point with a velocity v_1. Show that

PROBLEM 5.1.12

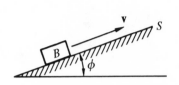

$$\left(\frac{v_1}{v_0}\right)^2 = \frac{1 - \mu \cot \phi}{1 + \mu \cot \phi}$$

A simple pendulum consists of a point of mass m at the end of a weightless cord of length l.
(a) What is the angular momentum of the pendulum with respect to the point of suspension at O?
(b) Determine the relation between the rate of change of angular momentum and the angular displacement θ.

PROBLEM 5.1.13

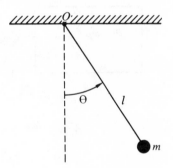

Section 5.2 Motion of a system

Two small spheres (considered to be particles), each of mass m, are free to move on a light rod as shown. The rod rotates in a frictionless bearing about a vertical axis. When each sphere is located a distance $r = r_0$ from the vertical axis, the angular speed of the rod is $\omega = \omega_0$. Each sphere is now moved radially inward to a distance $r = r_1$. What is the angular speed ω_1 of the rod?

SAMPLE PROBLEM

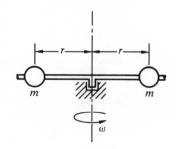

Solution

The angular momentum of the system about the vertical axis is $h = 2mr^2\omega$. Since the resultant force applied to each particle is radial, the moments of these forces about the vertical vanish; hence, $h = $ constant.

$$h_0 = 2mr_0{}^2\omega_0 = h_1 = 2mr_1{}^2\omega_1$$

$$\omega_1 = \omega_0\left(\frac{r_0}{r_1}\right)^2$$

SAMPLE PROBLEM

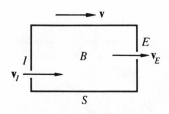

Consider a system of particles B which is enclosed by a surface S having two openings, I and E. The mass of the system varies because particles enter the system at I, while particles leave at E. The velocity of the mass center of B is $\mathbf{v}$. The velocity of the entering particles is $\mathbf{v}_I$ and that of the leaving particles is $\mathbf{v}_E$. Derive the equation of motion of the mass center of system B. Neglect the velocity of the particles of the system relative to its mass center. Apply the result to the case of a rocket.

Solution

For a system of *constant* mass

$$\mathbf{F} = \frac{d\mathbf{P}}{dt}$$

where $\mathbf{F} = $ resultant external force
$\mathbf{P} = $ linear momentum of the system

At time t: At time $t + \Delta t$:

    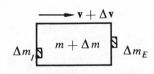

where $\Delta m_I = $ mass of particles entering in Δt
$\Delta m_E = $ mass of particles leaving in Δt

Considering the system of constant mass to consist of the particles in B at time t, and neglecting the variation in velocity of the particles in B, we have

76

$$\mathbf{P}(t) = m\mathbf{v}$$

$$\mathbf{P}(t + \Delta t) = (m + \Delta m)(\mathbf{v} + \Delta\mathbf{v}) + \Delta m_E \mathbf{v}_E - \Delta m_I \mathbf{v}_I$$

$$\Delta\mathbf{P} = m\mathbf{v} + m\,\Delta\mathbf{v} + \Delta m\mathbf{v} + \Delta m\,\Delta\mathbf{v} + \Delta m_E \mathbf{v}_E$$
$$- \Delta m_I \mathbf{v}_I - m\mathbf{v}$$

Also, $\Delta m = \Delta m_I - \Delta m_E$; hence

$$\frac{d\mathbf{P}}{dt} = m\frac{d\mathbf{v}}{dt} + \frac{dm_E}{dt}(\mathbf{v}_E - \mathbf{v}) - \frac{dm_I}{dt}(\mathbf{v}_I - \mathbf{v}) = \mathbf{F}$$

$$m\frac{d\mathbf{v}}{dt} = \mathbf{F} + \frac{dm_I}{dt}(\mathbf{v}_I - \mathbf{v}) - \frac{dm_E}{dt}(\mathbf{v}_E - \mathbf{v})$$

In the case of a rocket,

$$\frac{dm_I}{dt} = 0 \qquad \text{and} \qquad \frac{dm_E}{dt} = -\frac{dm}{dt}$$

$$m\frac{d\mathbf{v}}{dt} = \mathbf{F} + \frac{dm}{dt}(\mathbf{v}_E - \mathbf{v}) = \mathbf{F} + \mathbf{T}$$

where $\mathbf{T}$ = thrust. For rectilinear motion

$$m\frac{dv}{dt} = F - \frac{dm}{dt}v_e$$

where exit speed

$$v_e = v_E - v > 0$$

Note that

$$T = -\frac{dm}{dt}v_e > 0 \qquad \text{since} \qquad \frac{dm}{dt} < 0$$

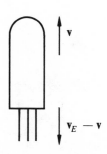

A uniform rectangular box rests on the flat bed of a truck. The coefficient of friction between the truck and the box is $\mu = 0.3$, and the box weighs 322 lb. Determine the maximum acceleration that the truck can attain so that the box neither slips nor tips.

PROBLEM 5.2.1

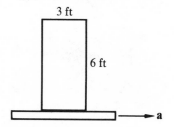

3 ft

6 ft

Motion of a system

77

PROBLEM 5.2.2

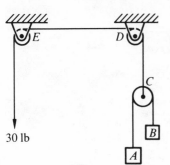

30 lb

A 30-lb force is applied to a flexible cord which passes over two light pulleys E and D. The other end is attached to a third light pulley at C, which in turn supports weights $A = 40$ lb and $B = 30$ lb as shown. Neglecting friction and assuming the cords are weightless, determine the accelerations of weights A and B.

PROBLEM 5.2.3

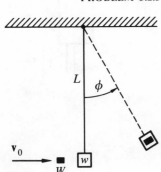

A projectile of weight $W = 0.1$ lb moving horizontally strikes and is embedded in a block of weight $w = 50$ lb. The block is attached to a light string of length $L = 20$ ft whose other end is fixed. If the maximum angular displacement of the string is 0.2 radians, what is the speed v_0 of the projectile prior to striking the block? Is energy conserved? Explain your answer. (Treat the block as a particle).

PROBLEM 5.2.4

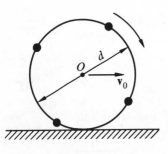

Four particles, each of mass m, are rigidly attached at 90° intervals around a massless wheel of diameter d which rolls without slipping on a horizontal plane. The velocity of the center is v_0. Find the angular momentum of the system with respect to
(a) The instantaneous center of zero velocity of the system;
(b) The mass center O.

PROBLEM 5.2.5

A system of two particles moves in a plane. One particle has mass m_1; when its position is

$$\mathbf{r}_1 = 2\mathbf{i} + 3\mathbf{j}$$

its velocity is

Methods of plane dynamics

$$\mathbf{v}_1 = 4\mathbf{i} + \mathbf{j}$$

The other particle has mass $m_2 = 2m_1$; at the same instant its position is

$$\mathbf{r}_2 = \mathbf{i} + 4\mathbf{j}$$

and its velocity is

$$\mathbf{v}_2 = 2\mathbf{i} - 3\mathbf{j}$$

Determine:
(a) The linear momentum of the system relative to the $\mathbf{i},\mathbf{j}$-coordinate system;
(b) The angular momentum of the system with respect to the origin O of the $\mathbf{i},\mathbf{j}$-coordinate system.

A 10-lb block starts from rest and slides down the inclined plane as shown. After moving through a distance d it strikes the end of a linear spring and compresses it 3 in. before coming to rest. If the coefficient of friction is 0.2 and spring constant $k = 15$ lb/in., determine the distance d.

PROBLEM 5.2.6

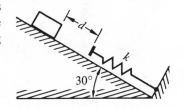

Two particles of mass m_1 and m_2, respectively, move solely under the action of forces exerted by one particle on the other and directed along the line joining the particles. Show that
(a) The particles move in a plane;
(b) The mass center of the system is fixed relative to some inertial coordinate system.

PROBLEM 5.2.7

Two small spheres S_1 and S_2, of weights 6 lb and 15 lb, respectively, slide without friction on the vertical L-frame shown. Sphere S_1 is connected by a linear spring of constant $k = 10$ lb/ft and unstretched length 2 ft to fixed point O and by a light bar of length 4 ft to sphere S_2. If the system is released from rest in the position shown, determine the speed of the spheres when S_1 has reached a position 1 ft to the left of the initial position.

PROBLEM 5.2.8

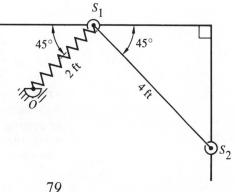

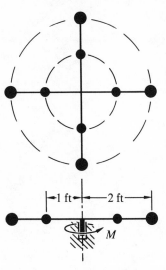

PROBLEM 5.2.9 Eight small spheres are rigidly attached to a light cross bar as shown. Each outer sphere weighs 1 lb, and each inner sphere weighs 0.75 lb. The cross bar is free to rotate about a vertical axis in a frictionless bearing. A moment about the vertical axis $M = 6t$ lb-ft (with t in sec) is applied to the cross bar which is initially at rest. Determine the speed of each ball when $t = 2$ sec.

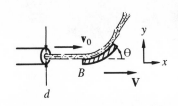

PROBLEM 5.2.10 The model of a steam turbine wheel may be represented by the system shown in which a single blade B diverts a fluid stream emerging from a nozzle through angle θ. The diameter of the nozzle is d, the density of the fluid is ρ, and the initial velocity of the fluid is $\mathbf{v}_0$.
(a) Determine the force components in the x and y directions required to hold the blade in a stationary position.
(b) Determine these force components when the blade has a uniform velocity $\mathbf{V}$ (less than $\mathbf{v}_0$) in the direction of $\mathbf{v}_0$.
(c) Determine the power developed by this blade. What speed V will yield the maximum power for given values of ρ, d, v_0, and θ?

PROBLEM 5.2.11 A rocket of initial mass m_0 and constant exit speed v_e ascends vertically from its rest position on the surface of the earth. Thrust ceases at time t_b when the mass of the rocket is m_b. Assuming a constant gravitational acceleration g and neglecting air resistance, determine the speed of the rocket when thrust ceases. If the thrust is constant, what is the altitude of the rocket when thrust ceases?

Methods of plane dynamics

Section 5.3 Moving frames of reference

A bead of mass m slides without friction in a tube which is
pinned to a fixed point O and rotates with constant angular
velocity ω. When $r = 2$ ft, the angular velocity of the tube
$\omega = 5$ radians/sec counterclockwise, the velocity of the bead
relative to the tube is 4 ft/sec outward, and its relative acceleration is 3 ft/sec² outward. Find the absolute acceleration of
the bead at this instant. What corresponding force acts on
the bead if the bead weighs 1 lb?

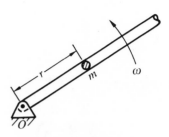

Solution

Let Oxy be a coordinate system fixed in the tube. The absolute
acceleration **a** is given by Eq. (5.314) of Synge and Griffith as

$$\mathbf{a} = (\ddot{x} - 2\omega\dot{y} - \omega^2 x)\mathbf{i} + (\ddot{y} + 2\omega\dot{x} - \omega^2 y)\mathbf{j}$$

where $\dot{x} = 4$ ft/sec

$\ddot{x} = 3$ ft/sec²

$y = \dot{y} = \ddot{y} = 0$

$\omega = 5$ radians/sec

$x = r = 2$ ft

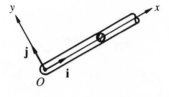

Hence

$$\mathbf{a} = (3 - 0 - 50)\mathbf{i} + (0 + 40 - 0)\mathbf{j} = -47\mathbf{i} + 40\mathbf{j} \text{ ft/sec}^2$$

Since $\mathbf{F} = m\mathbf{a}$, and $m = 1/32.2$ slug,

$$\mathbf{F} = \frac{1}{32.2}(-47\mathbf{i} + 40\mathbf{j}) \text{ lb}$$

Derive the relation between the expressions for velocity and
acceleration of a point in planar motion as seen by two
observers moving in the plane.

Moving frames of reference   *81*

Solution

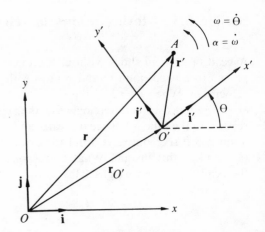

Consider two coordinate systems Oxy and $O'x'y'$ in general planar motion. Let $\mathbf{k}$ be the unit vector normal to the plane of motion. The position of point A relative to Oxy is given by

$$\mathbf{r} = x\mathbf{i} + y\mathbf{j}$$

and its position relative to $O'x'y'$ is given by

$$\mathbf{r}' = x'\mathbf{i}' + y'\mathbf{j}'$$

where

$$\mathbf{r} = \mathbf{r}_{O'} + \mathbf{r}$$

The time rate of change of $\mathbf{r}$ as seen by the observer in Oxy is

$$\frac{d\mathbf{r}}{dt} = \frac{d\mathbf{r}_{O'}}{dt} + \frac{d\mathbf{r}}{dt}$$

so that the velocity of A, $\mathbf{v} = \dfrac{d\mathbf{r}}{dt}$, relative to Oxy, is

$$\mathbf{v} = \mathbf{v}_{O'} + (\dot{x}'\mathbf{i}' + \dot{y}'\mathbf{j}') + x'\frac{d\mathbf{i}'}{dt} + y'\frac{d\mathbf{j}'}{dt}$$

where

$$\mathbf{v}_{O'} = \frac{d\mathbf{r}_{O'}}{dt}$$

The rates of change of the unit vectors $\mathbf{i}'$ and $\mathbf{j}'$ are determined from the figures as

$$\frac{d\mathbf{i}'}{dt} = \omega\mathbf{j}' = \boldsymbol{\omega} \times \mathbf{i}' \qquad \frac{d\mathbf{j}'}{dt} = -\omega\mathbf{i}' = \boldsymbol{\omega} \times \mathbf{j}'$$

where

$$\boldsymbol{\omega} = \omega\mathbf{k} \qquad \omega = \dot{\theta}$$

Methods of plane dynamics

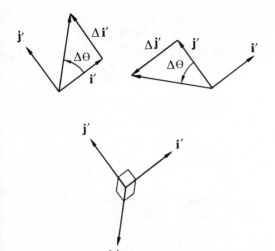

Thus
$$\mathbf{v} = \mathbf{v}_{O'} + \mathbf{v}' + \boldsymbol{\omega} \times \mathbf{r}'$$

where $\mathbf{v}' = \dot{x}'\mathbf{i}' + \dot{y}'\mathbf{j}'$ is the velocity of A relative to $O'x'y'$.

The acceleration of point A relative to Oxy is

$$\mathbf{a} = \frac{d\mathbf{v}}{dt} = \frac{d\mathbf{v}_{O'}}{dt} + (\ddot{x}'\mathbf{i}' + \ddot{y}'\mathbf{j}') + \dot{x}'\frac{d\mathbf{i}'}{dt}$$

$$+ \dot{y}'\frac{d\mathbf{j}'}{dt} + \frac{d\boldsymbol{\omega}}{dt} \times \mathbf{r}' + \boldsymbol{\omega} \times \frac{d\mathbf{r}'}{dt}$$

$$= \mathbf{a}_{O'} + \mathbf{a}' + 2\boldsymbol{\omega} \times \mathbf{v}' + \boldsymbol{\omega} \times (\boldsymbol{\omega} \times \mathbf{r}') + \boldsymbol{\alpha} \times \mathbf{r}'$$

where
$$\frac{d\mathbf{r}'}{dt} = (\dot{x}'\mathbf{i}' + \dot{y}'\mathbf{j}') + \boldsymbol{\omega} \times \mathbf{r}' = \mathbf{v}' + \boldsymbol{\omega} \times \mathbf{r}'$$

$$\boldsymbol{\alpha} = \frac{d\boldsymbol{\omega}}{dt}$$

The terms on the right-hand side of the acceleration equation are the acceleration of O' relative to Oxy, the acceleration of A relative to $O'x'y'$, the Coriolis acceleration, the centrifugal acceleration, and the contribution of the angular acceleration of $O'x'y'$, respectively.

Using the result of the second sample problem at the beginning of this section, derive Eq. (5.314) of Synge and Griffith. **PROBLEM 5.3.1**

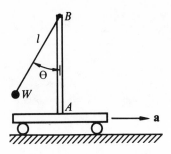

PROBLEM 5.3.2 A pole AB is fixed to a coaster moving with constant acceleration $\mathbf{a}$ on a horizontal plane as shown. A bob of weight W is attached at B by means of a light flexible cable of length l. Find the value of the constant angle θ between the pole and the cable.

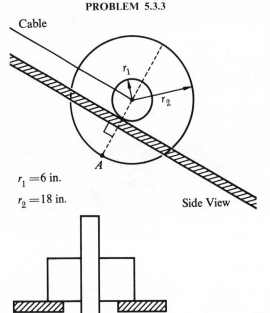

PROBLEM 5.3.3

Cable

$r_1 = 6$ in.

$r_2 = 18$ in.

Side View

View looking up plane

A cable is being used to lower a wheel which rolls on its hubs down the incline as shown. Determine the velocity and acceleration of point A at the instant when the center of the wheel has a velocity of 6 ft/sec and an acceleration of 8 ft/sec^2, both downhill.

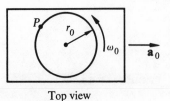

PROBLEM 5.3.4 A turntable of radius r_0 rotates without friction about a shaft which is rigidly attached to the horizontal flat bed of a truck moving at constant acceleration $\mathbf{a}_0$. If the turntable rotates with constant angular speed ω_0 relative to the truck, determine the acceleration of a point on the periphery of the turntable.

Top view

Methods of plane dynamics

Suppose an insect walks in an outward direction along a radial line on the turntable of Prob. 5.3.4. If the insect's speed relative to the turntable is $v_0 = $ constant, what is its acceleration relative to the road?

PROBLEM 5.3.5

Arm OA rotates in a horizontal plane about point O, while the disk pinned at A rotates in the same plane about its axis. If the disk has an angular velocity $\omega = 2$ radians/sec counterclockwise relative to arm OA, and the arm has an angular velocity of $\Omega = 3$ radians/sec counterclockwise, calculate the velocity and acceleration of the points A, B, and C at the instant shown in the figure.

PROBLEM 5.3.6

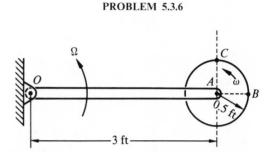

A bead of mass 0.01 slug can move along the circular-shaped wire AC, while the straight wire AB, whose position is determined by the angle ϕ, is pinned at A and threaded through the bead as shown. When $\phi = 45°$, the angular speed of AB is $\dot\phi = 2$ radians/sec, and $\ddot\phi = 5$ radians/sec². Find the velocity and acceleration of the bead in
(a) Polar coordinates with respect to A;
(b) Normal and tangential components with respect to O. (Hint: $\theta = 2\phi$.) Find the force on the bead at this instant.

PROBLEM 5.3.7

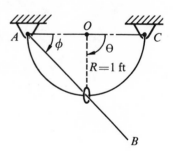

The slider-crank mechanism shown consists of a light crank OB and connecting rod AB, and a piston with a diameter $d = 4$ in. weighing 6 lb. The crank has a constant angular velocity $\omega = 100$ radians/sec counterclockwise. At the instant shown, the gas pressure p is 600 lb/in.² Determine the force acting on wrist pin A.

PROBLEM 5.3.8

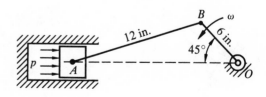

Moving frames of reference

PROBLEM 5.3.9 Consider the slider-crank mechanism discussed in Prob. 5.3.8. The crank now has a variable angular velocity. At the instant shown, its angular velocity is $\omega = 200$ radians/sec and its angular acceleration $\dot{\omega} = 2,000$ radians/sec^2, both counterclockwise, while the gas pressure p is 600 lb/in^2. Determine the force acting on wrist pin A.

PROBLEM 5.3.10 A rigid 10-ft rod rotates in a plane about an axis through one end at a constant angular velocity of 4 radians/sec counterclockwise. A ring of mass 2 slugs is moved outward along the rod at a constant speed of 4 ft/sec relative to the rod. Find the force acting on the ring at the instant it reaches the end of the rod.

PROBLEM 5.3.11

The shaper mechanism shown consists of two links AB and CD, each of negligible mass, and a slider B weighing 20 lb. At the instant shown, link AB has an angular velocity $\omega = 12$ radians/sec counterclockwise and zero angular acceleration $\dot{\omega}$. Determine the force acting on slider B.

At the instant shown, crank OA of the four-bar linkage has an angular velocity $\omega = 20$ radians/sec and an angular acceleration $\dot{\omega} = 50$ radians/sec^2, both clockwise. A uniform sphere weighing 5 lb is attached to the end B of link BC. Neglecting the weights of the links, determine the force acting on the sphere.

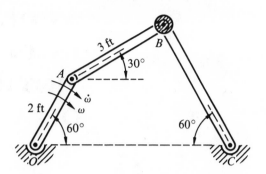

Due to the earth's rotation the weight of a body (i.e., the force required to keep the body at rest relative to the earth) varies with the latitude λ of the body's location. Assuming a spherically symmetrical earth, what would the angular speed Ω (in radians/sec) of the earth have to be in order that a body be weightless at the Equator?

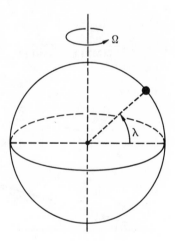

Moving frames of reference

APPLICATIONS
IN PLANE DYNAMICS:
MOTION
OF A PARTICLE

Section 6.1   Projectiles without resistance

A projectile is fired from point O on an incline of angle β to the horizontal as shown. If the initial velocity $\mathbf{v}_0$ is inclined at an angle α from the horizontal, determine α such that the projectile will strike the incline at the farthest possible point B from O. Neglect air resistance.

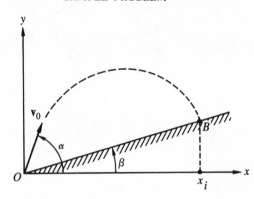

Solution

The projectile moves according to the equations

$$x = (v_0 \cos \alpha)t \\ y = (v_0 \sin \alpha)t - \frac{gt^2}{2} \Bigg\}$$ (1)

Eliminating time from Eqs. (1) gives the equation of the trajectory

88

$$y = x \tan \alpha - \frac{gx^2}{2v_0{}^2 \cos^2 \alpha} \qquad (2)$$

The equation of line OB can be written as

$$y = \frac{dy}{dx} \, x = (\tan \beta)x$$

Substituting this value of y in (2) gives the value of $x = x_i$ at impact:

$$x \tan \beta = x \tan \alpha - \frac{gx^2}{2v_0{}^2 \cos^2 \alpha}$$

whence $\qquad x_i = (\tan \alpha - \tan \beta)\dfrac{2v_0{}^2}{g} \cos^2 \alpha$

or $\qquad x_i = \dfrac{v_0{}^2}{g}(\sin 2\alpha - 2 \cos^2 \alpha \tan \beta) \qquad (3)$

To maximize the value of x_i it is necessary that $dx_i/d\alpha = 0$; from this relation we then determine α, which is the required angle. Note that maximizing x_i is equivalent to maximizing distance $\overline{OB}$, since $x_i = \overline{OB} \cos \beta$.

$$\frac{dx_i}{d\alpha} = \frac{v_0{}^2}{g}(2 \cos 2\alpha + 2 \sin 2\alpha \tan \beta) = 0$$

whence $\qquad \cot 2\alpha = - \tan \beta$

Thus $\qquad 2\alpha = \dfrac{\pi}{2} + \beta \qquad$ (rejecting $\dfrac{3\pi}{2} + \beta$)

and so $\qquad \alpha = \dfrac{\pi}{4} + \dfrac{\beta}{2}$

To check if this value of α yields a maximum of x_i, we form

$$\frac{d^2 x_i}{d\alpha^2} = 4\,\frac{v_0{}^2}{g}\,(\,-\sin 2\alpha + \cos 2\alpha \tan \beta)\big|_{2\alpha = \pi/2 + \beta}$$

$$= \frac{-4v_0{}^2}{g \cos \beta} < 0$$

which shows that we have a maximum.

PROBLEM 6.1.1 Two balls are thrown vertically upward along the same line and with the same initial velocity $\mathbf{v}_0$. If the second ball is thrown T sec after the first, find the height h above their common release point at which the balls meet.

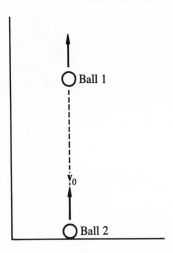

PROBLEM 6.1.2 A projectile is launched with an initial velocity of 500 ft/sec at an inclination of $30°$ to the horizontal.
(a) Find the position of the projectile after 5 sec.
(b) What is its velocity at this instant?
(c) Find the radius of curvature of its trajectory at the highest point. Neglect air resistance.

Motion of a particle

An airplane traveling at 500 mph is flying horizontally at a 10,000-foot elevation when it releases a small stone. Neglecting air resistance, determine the length $\overline{OB}$ of the horizontal projection of the stone's trajectory. What is the velocity of the stone when it hits the ground?

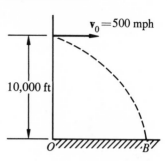

A ball is thrown from point A on a plane inclined at an angle of 30° to the horizontal. Find the initial velocity required to cause the ball to hit the plane at a point 100 ft down the plane. Neglect air resistance.

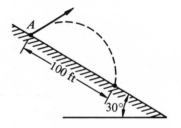

Neglecting air resistance, how far can a ball be thrown in a horizontal tunnel 20 ft in diameter without striking the top of the tunnel, if the ball's initial speed is 40 ft/sec?

If a person can throw a ball 100 yd when he tries for maximum range, how high could he throw it? Neglect air resistance.

A target is placed at a horizontal range of 1,000 yd from a mortar which fires projectiles with initial speed of 300 ft/sec. Find the angle (or angles) of the mortar tube with respect to the horizontal so that the projectiles will hit the target. Neglect air resistance.

Projectiles without resistance   *91*

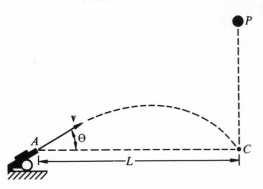

A ball at rest is released from point P at the instant a bullet leaves the muzzle of a gun located at point A. The gun barrel is inclined to the horizontal at angle θ, the bullet has a muzzle speed v, and the horizontal distance from the gun to the line of fall of the ball is L. If the bullet hits the ball at point C on a level with the muzzle of the gun, what is the value of angle θ? Is it a unique value? At what height(s) may the release point P be placed in order that impact occurs for given v and L?

PROBLEM 6.1.9

A bomber flies at a speed of 400 mph and an elevation of 8,000 ft in enemy territory, when the navigator observes a locomotive traveling at a constant speed of 40 mph in a direction at right angles to the path of the airplane. At this instant, $a = 20,000$ ft and $b = 1,600$ ft. Assuming that the speed of the locomotive remains constant, that the plane does not change its course, and that air resistance can be neglected, what must be the constant acceleration of the airplane so that a bomb dropped from it will hit the locomotive? What is the speed of the plane at the instant of release?

Section 6.2 Projectiles with resistance

SAMPLE PROBLEM

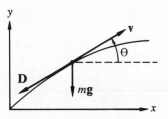

A projectile moves through the atmosphere. If the air resistance $\mathbf{D}$ is directed opposite to the projectile's velocity $\mathbf{v}$ and is proportional to its speed, write the equations of motion and integrate them to determine the position as a function of time.

Motion of a particle

Solution

Let θ denote the angle between $\mathbf{v}$ and the horizontal. Then

$$m\ddot{x} = -D\cos\theta \qquad m\ddot{y} = -mg - D\sin\theta \qquad (1)$$

Let s denote distance measured along the trajectory, that is,

$$\cos\theta = \frac{dx}{ds} \qquad \sin\theta = \frac{dy}{ds} \qquad v = \frac{ds}{dt} = \dot{s}$$

Since $D = kv$, $k = $ const, and letting $\lambda = \dfrac{k}{m}$, Eqs. (1) become

$$\ddot{x} = -\lambda\dot{x} \qquad \ddot{y} = -g - \lambda\dot{y} \qquad (2)$$

subject to initial conditions

$$t = 0: \qquad x = y = 0$$
$$\dot{x} = v_0\cos\theta_0$$
$$\dot{y} = v_0\sin\theta_0$$

The first of Eqs. (2) is homogeneous. Its solution is of the form $x = a_1 + b_1 e^{-\lambda t}$ where a_1 and b_1 are constants. Upon use of the initial conditions, we find

$$a_1 = -b_1 = \frac{v_0\cos\theta_0}{\lambda}$$

The second of Eqs. (2) is nonhomogeneous. Its solution is of the form $y = a_2 + b_2 e^{-\lambda t} + ct$ where a_2, b_2, and c are constants. Constant c is found by substitution of the solution in the differential equation, whence

$$c = -\frac{g}{\lambda}$$

Then use of the initial conditions gives

$$a_2 = -b_2 = \frac{g}{\lambda^2} + \frac{v_0\sin\theta_0}{\lambda}$$

In the sample problem at the beginning of this section the force of air resistance D is assumed proportional to the speed v of a projectile; that is, $D = kv$ where $k = $ constant. If the weight of the projectile is mg, show that its terminal velocity (as time $t \to \infty$) is directed vertically downward and of magnitude mg/k.

PROBLEM 6.2.1

Projectiles with resistance

93

PROBLEM 6.2.2   A body of mass m is in rectilinear motion on a smooth horizontal table. The air resistance, $\mathbf{D}$, is directed opposite to the body's velocity, $\mathbf{v}$, and is proportional to the square of its speed; i.e., $D = kv^2$ and $k = $ constant. If $x = 0$ and $v = v_0$ when $t = 0$, where $v = dx/dt$, find x and v as functions of t.

PROBLEM 6.2.3   A projectile is fired with an initial velocity of magnitude $v_0 = 500$ ft/sec inclined at an angle $\theta_0 = 30°$ to the horizontal.
(a) Neglecting air resistance, compute the range of the projectile.
(b) Assuming that the air resistance is proportional to the projectile's speed v and that the proportionality constant $k = 0.05$ lb-sec^2/ft^2, compute the range.

PROBLEM 6.2.4   A particle weighing 1 lb is projected vertically upward with an initial speed $v_0 = 30$ ft/sec in a medium which opposes the motion with a force equal to $0.1v$ lb, where v is the instantaneous speed. Find the time for the particle to attain its peak height. How long will it take to fall from there back to the starting point?

PROBLEM 6.2.5   A body of mass m is released from rest and falls under gravity in a medium exerting a drag force proportional to the square of the speed. Determine the terminal velocity ($t \to \infty$).

PROBLEM 6.2.6   A projectile moves in a medium giving rise to a drag force proportional to the square of the speed. If the trajectory is very flat ($\sin \theta = \theta$, $\cos \theta = 1$, where θ is the angle of inclination of velocity to the horizontal), find the position of the projectile as a function of inclination angle θ and initial conditions.

PROBLEM 6.2.7   A projectile moves in a medium giving rise to a drag force proportional to the square of the speed. If the trajectory is very flat, namely, dy/dx may be neglected compared to unity, where dy/dx is the tangent of the trajectory, determine the position as a function of time and initial conditions.

Motion of a particle

Section 6.3   Harmonic oscillators

The system shown consists of a linear spring of constant k and unstretched length L, a light bar AB of length $2L$, and a small ball of mass m attached at point B. The spring is sufficiently weak so that the system is in stable equilibrium in the vertical position. Neglecting friction, determine the frequency of small oscillations.

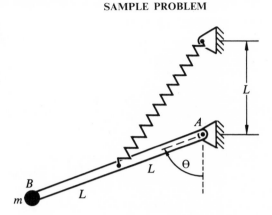

Solution

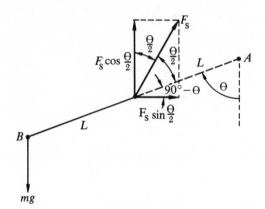

By the law of cosines, the change in length of the spring, δ, is given by

$$\delta = \sqrt{2L^2 + 2L^2 \cos \theta} - L = L(2 \cos \tfrac{1}{2}\theta - 1)$$

The spring force is

$$F_s = k\delta = kL(2 \cos \tfrac{1}{2}\theta - 1)$$

Method 1: By using the principle of angular momentum with respect to point A:

$$\dot{h}_A = N_A$$

Harmonic oscillators   *95*

$$4mL^2\ddot{\theta} = -2mgL \sin\theta + kL\ (2\cos\tfrac{1}{2}\theta - 1)$$

$$\times \left(L\cos\frac{\theta}{2} \sin\theta - L\sin\frac{\theta}{2} \cos\theta \right)$$

For small values of θ,

$$\sin\theta \approx \theta \qquad \sin\frac{\theta}{2} \approx \frac{\theta}{2} \qquad \cos\theta \approx \cos\frac{\theta}{2} \approx 1$$

Then
$$\ddot{\theta} + \frac{2mg - (kL/2)}{4mL}\theta = 0$$

This is the equation for simple harmonic motion with angular frequency

$$\omega = \sqrt{\frac{4mg - kL}{8mL}} \qquad \text{which requires } k < \frac{4mg}{L}$$

Method 2: Using the energy principle in the form $\dot{T} + \dot{V} = 0$:

$$T = \tfrac{1}{2}(4mL^2\dot{\theta}^2)$$

$$V - V(0) = 2mgL(1 - \cos\theta) + \tfrac{1}{2}k\delta^2$$

$$V(0) = \tfrac{1}{2}kL^2$$

$$V - V(0) = 2mgL(1 - \cos\theta) - 2kL^2 \cos\frac{\theta}{2}\left(1 - \cos\frac{\theta}{2}\right)$$

For small oscillations

$$1 - \cos\theta \approx \frac{\theta^2}{2} \qquad \cos\frac{\theta}{2} \approx 1 \qquad 1 - \cos\frac{\theta}{2} \approx \frac{\theta^2}{8}$$

and
$$V - V(0) \approx \tfrac{1}{2}(2mgL - \tfrac{1}{2}kL^2)\,\theta^2$$

$$\dot{T} + \dot{V} = [4mL^2\ddot{\theta} + (2mgL - \tfrac{1}{2}kL^2)\,\theta]\dot{\theta} = 0$$

$$\ddot{\theta} + \frac{2mg - kL/2}{4mL}\theta = 0 \qquad \omega = \sqrt{\frac{4mg - kL}{8mL}}$$

An air compressor with a total weight of 3,600 lb is actuated by a piston weighing 40 lb that executes simple harmonic motion with an amplitude $a = 8$ in. at a flywheel speed of 300 rpm. It is desired to design a spring-dashpot mounting system (vibration-isolating support) that will transmit a maximum force over the static weight of 400 lb to the foundation under normal operating conditions and, further, will limit the displacement of the compressor to 0.5 in. at the natural frequency of the system.

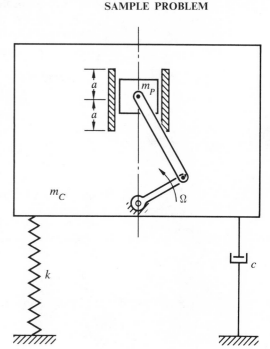

Solution

The equation of motion of the system is

$$(m_C - m_P)\ddot{x} + m_P\left(\ddot{x} + \frac{d^2}{dt^2} a \cos \Omega t\right) = -c\dot{x} - kx$$

where x is measured from the equilibrium position of the unforced system (free length of spring). Thus

$$m_C\ddot{x} + c\dot{x} + kx = m_P a \Omega^2 \cos \Omega t$$

The solution of this equation is given by the sum of the solution x_1 to the homogeneous equation and of a particular solution x_2.

x_1 is given by Eq. (6.330) of Synge and Griffith as

$$x_1 = Ce^{-ct/2m_C} \cos (qt - \phi) \qquad \text{(the transient solution)}$$

with

$$q \equiv \sqrt{\left|\left(\frac{c}{2m_C}\right)^2 - \left(\frac{k}{m_C}\right)^2\right|}$$

Harmonic oscillators   97 for the case of light damping $(c/2m < \omega)$, where $\omega \equiv \sqrt{k/m_C}$ is the natural frequency of the undamped system, and C and ϕ are constants determined from initial conditions. The particular solution will be assumed in the form

$$x_2 = A \cos \Omega t + B \sin \Omega t \qquad \text{(the steady state response)}$$

where A and B are to be determined so as to satisfy the original differential equation. Upon substitution of x_2 we obtain

$$(- m_C\Omega^2 A + cB\Omega + kA - m_p a\Omega^2) \cos \Omega t$$
$$+ (- m_C\Omega^2 B - cA\Omega + kB) \sin \Omega t = 0$$

and equating the coefficients of $\sin \Omega t$ and $\cos \Omega t$ to zero separately, we obtain

$$(- m_C\Omega^2 + k)A + cB\Omega = m_p a\Omega^2$$

$$- cA\Omega + (- m_C\Omega^2 + k)B = 0$$

so that, with $M \equiv \dfrac{m_P}{m_C}$,

$$A = \frac{m_p a\Omega^2(k - m_C\Omega^2)}{(k - m_C\Omega^2)^2 + c^2\Omega^2} = \frac{Ma\left(\dfrac{\Omega}{\omega}\right)^2\left(1 - \dfrac{\Omega^2}{\omega^2}\right)}{\left(1 - \dfrac{\Omega^2}{\omega^2}\right)^2 + \left(\dfrac{c}{\omega m_C}\right)^2\left(\dfrac{\Omega}{\omega}\right)^2}$$

$$B = \frac{c m_p a\Omega^3}{(k - m_C\Omega^2)^2 + c^2\Omega^2} = \frac{Ma\left(\dfrac{c}{\omega m_C}\right)\left(\dfrac{\Omega}{\omega}\right)^3}{\left(1 - \dfrac{\Omega^2}{\omega^2}\right)^2 + \left(\dfrac{c}{\omega m_C}\right)^2\left(\dfrac{\Omega}{\omega}\right)^2}$$

The equation for x_2 may also be written as

$$x_2 = E \cos (\Omega t - \eta)$$

where

$$\tan \eta = \frac{B}{A}$$

and $E = \sqrt{A^2 + B^2} = \dfrac{Ma\left(\dfrac{\Omega}{\omega}\right)^2}{\sqrt{\left(1 - \dfrac{\Omega^2}{\omega^2}\right)^2 + \left(\dfrac{\Omega}{\omega}\right)^2\left(\dfrac{c}{\omega m_C}\right)^2}}$

After a long time the transient solution becomes negligible and only the steady state solution is of importance. The

Motion of a particle

transmissibility is defined as the ratio of the force F_T transmitted to the foundation to the load F_0 applied to the system, the latter being $F_0 = m_p a \Omega^2$. The force transmitted to the foundation is due to the spring, kx_2, and the dashpot, $c\dot{x}_2$, so that

$$\frac{F_T}{F_0} = \frac{\sqrt{(kx_2)^2_{max} + (c\dot{x}_2)^2_{max}}}{m_p a \Omega^2} = \sqrt{\frac{1 + \left(\dfrac{c}{\omega m_c}\right)^2 \left(\dfrac{\Omega}{\omega}\right)^2}{\left(1 - \dfrac{\Omega^2}{\omega^2}\right)^2 + \left(\dfrac{c}{\omega m_c}\right)^2 \left(\dfrac{\Omega}{\omega}\right)^2}}$$

At resonance,

$$\Omega = \omega \qquad x_2 = E \cos(\Omega t - \eta) = \frac{M a \omega m_c}{c} \cos(\Omega t - \eta)$$

and

$$|x_2|_{max} = \frac{M a \omega m_c}{c} = \frac{m_p \omega a}{c}$$

Hence

$$c = \frac{m_p \omega a}{|x_2|_{max}} = \frac{40 \sqrt{\dfrac{k \times 32.2 \times 12}{3,600}} \times 8}{32.2 \times 12 \times 0.5}$$

$$= 0.542 \sqrt{k} \text{ lb-sec/in.} = 1.65\omega \text{ lb-sec/in.}$$

and

$$F_0 = m_p a \Omega^2 = \frac{40}{386} 8 \left(\frac{300}{60} 2\pi\right)^2 = 820 \text{ lb}$$

From the transmissibility equation, with $c/\omega m_c = 1.65/m_c = (1.65 \times 386)/3,600 = 0.177$, we have

$$\left(\frac{400}{820}\right)^2 \left[\left(1 - \frac{\Omega^2}{\omega^2}\right)^2 + \left(\frac{c}{\omega m_c}\right)^2 \left(\frac{\Omega}{\omega}\right)^2\right] = 1 + \left(\frac{c}{\omega m_c}\right)^2 \left(\frac{\Omega}{\omega}\right)^2$$

$$0.238 \left[1 - 1.969 \left(\frac{\Omega}{\omega}\right)^2 + \left(\frac{\Omega}{\omega}\right)^4\right] = 1 + 0.0313 \left(\frac{\Omega}{\omega}\right)^2$$

$$\left(\frac{\Omega}{\omega}\right)^2 = 3.06 \qquad \frac{\Omega}{\omega} = 1.751$$

$$\omega = \frac{300 \times 2\pi}{60 \times 1.751} = 17.95 \text{ radians/sec}$$

$$c = 1.65\omega = 29.6 \text{ lb-sec/in.}$$

$$k = m_c \omega^2 = \frac{3,600}{386}(17.95)^2 = 3,000 \text{ lb/in.}$$

What is the natural frequency of small oscillations of weight W, which is attached to the end of a uniform cantilever beam? Assume the weight of the beam to be small compared to W.

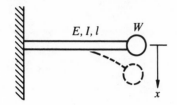

If the vertical wire is under tension T, what will be the natural frequency of small vibrations when the weight is displaced laterally?

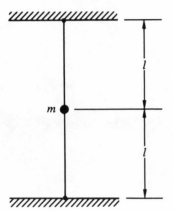

The differential equation for a single-degree-of-freedom undamped harmonic oscillator without any disturbing force is $m\ddot{x} + kx = 0$. Determine the equivalent spring constant k for the systems shown.

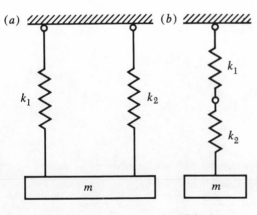

Motion of a particle

A U-tube of cross-sectional area A and in a vertical plane is partially filled with an incompressible liquid of density ρ. Determine the frequency of oscillations when the valve is quickly opened.

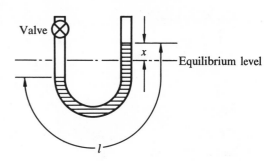

Determine the frequency of oscillation of a board of mass m and length L initially placed asymmetrically on two wheels of radius R, which rotate in opposite directions at the same angular speed ω. The distance between the centers of the wheels is $2l$ and the kinetic coefficient of friction is f_k.

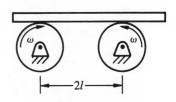

A rectangular block of wood with base area A, height h, and mass density ρ_b floats in water of density ρ_w. The block is depressed so as to be just submerged and is then released; calculate the frequency of the resulting oscillations. What are the major assumptions that must be made for this calculation to be correct?

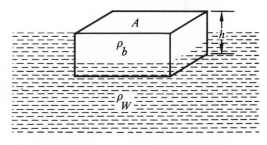

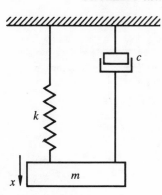

PROBLEM 6.3.7 A lightly damped harmonic oscillator is found to have a reduction of amplitude of its harmonic vibration of 20:1 after 12 cycles. The period of a cycle is 2 sec. If the mass of the system is 644 lb, determine
(a) The logarithmic decrement;
(b) The damping constant c in units of lb-sec/ft;
(c) The spring constant k of the system in units of lb/ft;
(d) The frequency p of the undamped oscillation of the system.

PROBLEM 6.3.8 Obtain an expression for the loss of energy per cycle for a lightly damped spring-mass system in terms of spring constant k, the logarithmic decrement, and amplitude A at the end of the cycle, which extends from peak to peak. Calculate the energy loss during the fifth cycle in Prob. 6.3.7.

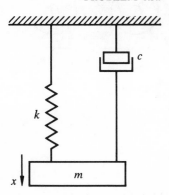

PROBLEM 6.3.9 A spring-mass system with critical damping has resistive force $F_d = c_c \dot{x}$, where $c_c = 2\sqrt{mk}$. This value of the damping constant divides the regions of *light* and *heavy* damping. Obtain the general solution for the free motion of such a system for initial conditions $x = x_0$ and $\dot{x} = \dot{x}_0$. Plot the result for (a) $x_0 > 0$, $\dot{x}_0 > 0$ and (b) $x_0 > 0$, $\dot{x}_0 < 0$. What is required for the system to cross its equilibrium position?

PROBLEM 6.3.10

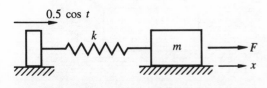

A mass m of 2 slugs is attached to a moving support by a spring with constant $k = 100$ lb/in. The support moves periodically with a horizontal displacement given by 0.5 cos t in. and the mass is subjected to a periodic force F of amplitude 10 lb and frequency $1/\pi$ cps. Find the steady state amplitude of oscillation of the mass. Neglect friction.

An electric motor is attached to the center of an elastic beam of negligible weight. The entire motor weighs 100 lb, the armature weighing 50 lb and having a mass center eccentric by 0.003 in. The motor causes a static deflection of 0.150 in. at the beam center. Determine the amplitude A of forced vibration of the beam center for a motor speed of 1,000 rpm.

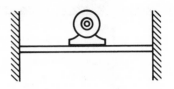

A spring-mounted trailer is pulled over a washboard road whose contour may be approximated by a sine or cosine function. The weight of the trailer is 1,000 lb; the weight of the wheels is negligible. During loading the trailer is observed to sag $\frac{1}{4}$ in. with each additional 250-lb load. If the trailer travels at 20 mph, what is the amplitude of vibration of the trailer? At what critical speed is this amplitude greatest? Assume that the wheels are always in contact with the road.

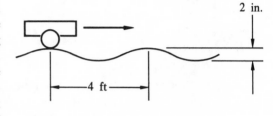

2 in.

4 ft

An undamped spring-mass system is subjected to the forced oscillation shown. If the system is at rest at time $t = 0$, determine the time history of the motion when $\Omega = p$, where p is the natural frequency of the system. If $m = 200$ lb-sec^2/ft, $k = 1,200$ lb/ft, and $F_0 = 50$ lb, what is the maximum time that the force can be applied under resonant conditions such that the amplitude of motion will not exceed the static deflection F_0/k by a factor of 10?

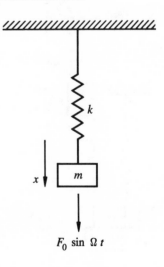

k

x m

$F_0 \sin \Omega t$

Harmonic oscillators

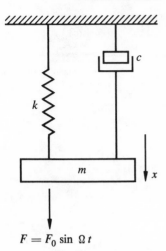

$F = F_0 \sin \Omega t$

PROBLEM 6.3.14 A system consists of a mass m, a linear spring of constant k, and a dashpot producing a viscous damping force $F_d = c\dot{x}$. The mass has an initial displacement and an initial speed $x = x_0$ and $\dot{x} = \dot{x}_0$, respectively. A disturbing force $F = F_0 \sin \Omega t$ is applied to the system. Derive an expression for the complete motion of the system.

PROBLEM 6.3.15 The magnification factor M of a spring-mass dashpot system subjected to forced oscillation is defined as the ratio of the amplitude of the forced oscillation to the deflection produced statically by the amplitude of the applied force. The critical damping constant $c_c = 2\sqrt{mk}$ is defined as the value of c dividing the regions of *light* and *heavy* damping. Derive expressions for the magnification factor and the tangent of the phase angle η for the system of Prob. 6.3.14 in terms of the ratios Ω/p and c/c_c, where p is the natural frequency of the undamped system and Ω is the forcing frequency. Plot M and $\tan \eta$ as functions of Ω/p for values of $c/c_c = 0$, $\frac{1}{4}, \frac{1}{2}, 1$, and 2 over the range $0 \leqslant (\Omega/p) \leqslant 3$.

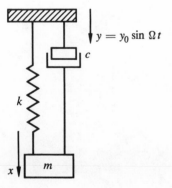

$y = y_0 \sin \Omega t$

PROBLEM 6.3.16 Determine the differential equation of motion and the expression for the forced oscillation of the linear spring-mass dashpot system shown. The motion of the supporting frame is given by $y = y_0 \sin \Omega t$. Determine dimensionless expressions for the magnification factor $M = x_{max}/y_0$, and for the tangent of the phase angle, and repeat the calculations of Prob. 6.3.15.

A motor mounted on a beam rotates at a constant angular speed with its center of gravity displaced distance e from the axis of rotation. The system is represented by the configuration shown. Repeat the derivation and calculations of Prob. 6.3.15, where the magnification factor is given by $M = x_{max}/e$.

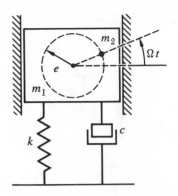

Derive the expression for the forced oscillation of the system shown. The motion of the platform is given by $y = y_0 \sin \Omega t$.

$$y = y_0 \sin \Omega t$$

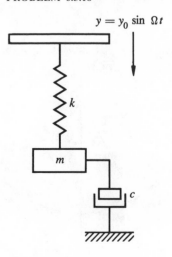

PROBLEM 6.3.19

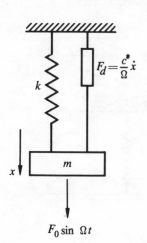

$F_d = \dfrac{c^*}{\Omega}\dot{x}$

k

x

m

$F_0 \sin \Omega t$

A spring-mass system with *structural* damping exhibits a resistive force $F_d = (c^*/\Omega)\dot{x}$, where c^* is a constant and Ω is the frequency of the forced oscillation resulting from a sinusoidal external force of amplitude F_0. Determine the expression for the motion of the forced oscillation. Determine expressions for the magnification factor $M = x_{max}/x_{st}$ and for the tangent of the phase angle η in terms of the frequency ratio Ω/p and a dimensionless damping constant $n = c^*/k$, where $x_{st} = F_0/k$ is the static deflection. Plot M and $\tan \eta$ in the range $0 \leqslant (\Omega/p) \leqslant 3$ for values of $n = 0, \frac{1}{4}, \frac{1}{2}, 1$ and 2.

PROBLEM 6.3.20

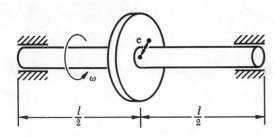

e

ω

$\dfrac{l}{2}$

$\dfrac{l}{2}$

If the center of mass of the uniform disk of radius r and mass m is distance e from the geometric center of the shaft, determine the critical speed of the shaft, neglecting its mass.

PROBLEM 6.3.21

If the disk rolls without slipping, determine the natural frequency of the system for small amplitude oscillations.

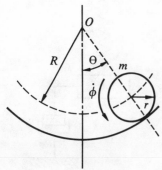

O

R

θ

m

$\dot{\phi}$

r

Determine the natural frequency of the system shown for small amplitude oscillations. The circular disk can rotate freely in the vertical plane about point O.

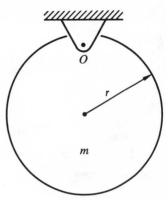

Section 6.4 General motion under a central force

Deduce the following properties of motion of a particle under the action of a force directed toward a fixed point:
(a) The angular momentum about the fixed point is constant;
(b) Motion takes place in a plane;
(c) The area swept out by the radius vector in unit time is constant.

Solution

$$\mathbf{F} = F(r)\mathbf{e}_r = m\frac{d\mathbf{v}}{dt}$$

Now form

$$\mathbf{r} \times \mathbf{F} = \mathbf{r} \times m\frac{d\mathbf{v}}{dt}$$

and since

$$\frac{d}{dt}(\mathbf{r} \times \mathbf{v}) = \mathbf{v} \times \mathbf{v} + \mathbf{r} \times \frac{d\mathbf{v}}{dt} = \mathbf{r} \times \frac{d\mathbf{v}}{dt}$$

and

$$\mathbf{r} \times \mathbf{F} = 0$$

we have

$$m\frac{d}{dt}(\mathbf{r} \times \mathbf{v}) = 0$$

that is,

$$\mathbf{r} \times m\mathbf{v} \equiv m\mathbf{h} = \text{const} \qquad (1)$$

General motion under a central force

107

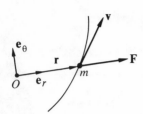

(a) From Eq. (1), it follows that the angular momentum about fixed point O is a constant.

(b) Furthermore, it follows from (1) that both $\mathbf{r}$ and $\mathbf{v}$ lie in the same invariant plane, which is the plane of motion.

Since
$$\mathbf{v} = \dot{r}\mathbf{e}_r + r\dot{\theta}\mathbf{e}_\theta$$

and
$$\mathbf{r} \times \mathbf{v} = \dot{r}\mathbf{r} \times \mathbf{e}_r + r^2\dot{\theta}\mathbf{e}_r \times \mathbf{e}_\theta = r^2\dot{\theta}\mathbf{e}_r \times \mathbf{e}_\theta$$

then
$$h \equiv |\mathbf{h}| = |\mathbf{r} \times \mathbf{v}| = r^2\dot{\theta} = \text{const} \qquad (2)$$

The increment of area swept out by the radius vector is

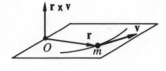

$$dA = \frac{1}{2}r^2\, d\theta$$

so that
$$\frac{dA}{dt} = \frac{1}{2}r^2\dot{\theta}$$

From Eq. (2) it follows that

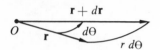

(c)
$$\frac{dA}{dt} = \frac{1}{2}h = \text{const}$$

PROBLEM 6.4.1   A particle of unit mass moves in a central force field with potential energy

$$V(r) = -k\frac{e^{-br}}{r}$$

where k and b are positive constants. Determine the differential equation of motion, and discuss qualitatively the nature of the motion.

PROBLEM 6.4.2   A particle of unit mass moves under the action of the central force

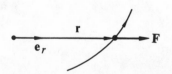

$$\mathbf{F} = \frac{k^2}{r^3}\mathbf{e}_r \qquad k = \text{const}$$

Determine the differential equation for the orbit, and describe the motion for the three possible cases that may arise. Are circular orbits possible under this central force?

108

Verify that differentiation with respect to θ of

$$\left(\frac{du}{d\theta}\right)^2 + u^2 = \frac{2(E - V)}{h^2}$$

$$[\text{Eq. (6.418) of Synge and Griffith}]$$

leads to the differential equation of the orbit of a point mass subject to an attractive central force per unit mass

$$\mathbf{P} = -\text{ grad } V$$

that is,

$$\frac{d^2u}{d\theta^2} + u = \frac{P}{h^2u^2} \qquad [\text{Eq. (6.414) of Synge and Griffith}]$$

where P is the inward component of $\mathbf{P}$.

A particle of unit mass moves under an attractive central force $\mathbf{F}$ which is proportional to the radial distance r from the center of attraction; that is, $\mathbf{F} = -k^2\mathbf{r}$, where $k =$ constant. Prove that the force field is conservative and that the potential energy of the particle $V = \frac{1}{2}k^2r^2$. Where is the datum of zero potential energy?

Derive an expression for the speed v of the particle discussed in Prob. 6.4.4.

What is the equation for the central attractive force $\mathbf{F}(r)$ for which particles of unit mass in all circular orbits have the same angular momentum $\mathbf{h}$?

What is the central force required so that a particle subjected to it will travel in the circle with the center of the force located on the trajectory?

A particle travels in a circular path subject to a central force $\mathbf{F}(r)$ of magnitude

$$F(r) = \frac{a}{r^2}e^{-br}$$

where a and b are positive constants. What is the stability of small deviations from the path?

Section 6.5 Planetary orbits

What is the energy E of a comet of mass m_1 subject to the attraction of the sun? If the comet is assumed to be at rest when it is an infinite distance from the sun, show that its speed v as a function of radial distance r is given by

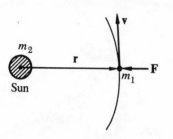

$$v = \sqrt{\frac{2\mu}{r}}$$

where $\mu = Gm_2$

G = universal gravitational constant

m_2 = mass of sun

Solution

$$\mathbf{F} = -\frac{\mu m_1}{r^2}\frac{\mathbf{r}}{r}$$

Taking the datum for zero potential energy at infinity, the potential energy is given by

$$V(\infty) - V(r) = \int_r^\infty \mathbf{F} \cdot d\mathbf{r}$$

$$= \int_r^\infty -\frac{\mu m_1}{r^2}\, dr = \frac{\mu m_1}{r} \qquad V(\infty) = 0$$

that is, $$V(r) = -\frac{\mu m_1}{r}$$

and the total energy

$$E = T + V = \frac{1}{2}m_1 v^2 - \frac{\mu m_1}{r}$$

where T is the kinetic energy.

If $v = 0$ at $r = \infty$, then $E = 0$ and

$$v = \sqrt{\frac{2\mu}{r}}$$

An artificial earth satellite is injected into its orbit with a horizontal velocity of 20,000 mph at an altitude of 400 miles. Assume the earth to be spherically symmetrical and of radius 4,000 miles.

Motion of a particle

(a) Compute angular momentum per unit mass h, constant $\mu = GM$ (where G = universal gravitational constant and M = mass of the earth), and eccentricity of the orbit e.
(b) Compute the maximum distance of the satellite from the surface of the earth (apogee).
(c) What horizontal velocity v_0 would the satellite have to have at an altitude of 400 miles in order to move in a parabolic orbit?

Solution

(a) The constant angular momentum per unit mass

$$h = r^2\dot\theta = r_0 v_0 = 4{,}400 \times 5{,}280 \, \frac{20{,}000 \times 5{,}280}{60 \times 60}$$

Therefore, $\quad h = 6.8 \times 10^{11} \text{ ft}^2/\text{sec}$

To find $\mu = GM$, where M is the mass of the earth, consider a mass of 1 slug at the surface of the earth and apply Newton's law $\mathbf{F} = m\mathbf{a}$, that is,

$$\mathbf{F} = \frac{GMm}{r^2} = mg \qquad \text{where } g = 32.2 \text{ ft/sec}^2$$

Thus $\mu = r^2 g = (4{,}000 \times 5{,}280)^2 \, 32.2 = 14.4 \times 10^{15} \text{ ft}^3/\text{sec}^2$
To find e, consider Eqs. (6.509) and (6.510) of Synge and Griffith:

$$\frac{1}{r} = u = \frac{1}{l}(1 + e \cos\theta)$$

$$l = \frac{h^2}{\mu}$$

so that $\qquad\qquad e \cos\theta = \dfrac{h^2 - r\mu}{r\mu} \qquad\qquad (1)$

Now consider Eq. (6.505) of Synge and Griffith, and evaluate the constant C using the initial conditions $u = 1/r_0 = 1/(4{,}400 \times 5{,}280)$ when $\theta = 0$, so that

$$C = \frac{1}{r_0} - \frac{\mu}{h^2} = \frac{h^2 - r_0\mu}{r_0 h^2} = 0.11 \times 10^{-7} \text{ ft}^{-1} \qquad (2)$$

Comparing (1) and (2), we see that

$$e = C\frac{h^2}{\mu} = \frac{(0.11 \times 10^{-7})(6.8 \times 10^{11})^2}{14.4 \times 10^{15}} = 0.35 \qquad (3)$$

Since $e < 1$, the trajectory is an ellipse, and Eq. (6.505) can be used to write the trajectory equation as

$$u = \frac{1}{r} = 0.32 \times 10^{-7} + 0.11 \times 10^{-7} \cos \theta$$

(b) The maximum distance (apogee) occurs when $\theta = \pi$, so that

$$\frac{1}{r_{max}} = (0.32 - 0.11) \times 10^{-7} = 0.21 \times 10^{-7} \text{ ft}^{-1}$$

$$r_{max} = 9{,}000 \text{ miles} \rightarrow \text{maximum altitude} = 5{,}000 \text{ miles}$$

(c) For a parabolic orbit $e = 1.0$. At $\theta = 0$, we have, from (2) and (3), that

$$e = C \frac{h^2}{\mu} = \left(\frac{1}{r_0} - \frac{\mu}{r_0{}^2 v_0{}^2}\right) \frac{r_0{}^2 v_0{}^2}{\mu}$$

Therefore

$$e = 1 = \frac{r_0 v_0{}^2}{\mu} - 1$$

that is,

$$v_0 = \sqrt{\frac{2\mu}{r_0}}$$

$$v_0 = 35{,}200 \text{ ft/sec} = 24{,}000 \text{ mph}$$

SAMPLE PROBLEM The shape (eccentricity e) and orientation (polar angle θ measured from line of closest approach $r = r_{min}$) of a Keplerian orbit may be computed in terms of the velocity of the orbiting body and its distance from the attractive center:

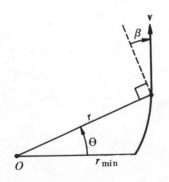

$$e^2 = \left(\frac{rv^2}{\mu} - 1\right)^2 \cos^2 \beta + \sin^2 \beta \qquad (1)$$

$$\tan \theta = \frac{\dfrac{rv^2}{\mu} \sin \beta \cos \beta}{\dfrac{rv^2}{\mu} \cos^2 \beta - 1} \qquad (2)$$

where $\mu = GM$

G = universal gravitational constant

M = mass of attracting body

112

A satellite is launched into an orbit about the earth. At burnout of the booster rocket, radar measurements show that

$$r = r_0 = 4{,}400 \text{ miles}$$

$$\beta = \beta_0 = 0$$

$$v = v_0 = 18{,}000 \text{ mph}$$

Compute the maximum and minimum altitudes of the satellite.

Solution

Since

$$r_{max} = \frac{h^2}{\mu(1 - e)} \qquad r_{min} = \frac{h^2}{\mu(1 + e)}$$

where $h = rv \cos \beta = \text{const}$, we must determine μ and e.
The force per unit mass is

$$F = -\frac{GM}{r^2} = -\frac{\mu}{r^2}$$

At the surface of the earth

$$F = g \cong 32 \text{ ft/sec}^2$$

$$r \cong 4{,}000 \text{ miles}$$

whence $\quad\quad \mu \cong 14.4 \times 10^{15} \text{ ft}^3/\text{sec}^2$

Also, since $\beta = 0$ at burnout,

$$h = r_0 v_0 = 6.14 \times 10^{11} \text{ ft}^2/\text{sec}$$

Using Eq. (1) we get

$$e = 0.135$$

so that

$r_{max} = 5{,}780 \text{ miles} \rightarrow \text{maximum altitude} = 1{,}780 \text{ miles}$

$r_{min} = 4{,}400 \text{ miles} \rightarrow \text{minimum altitude} = 400 \text{ miles}$

Planetary orbits

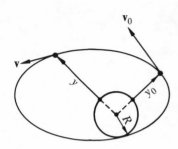

PROBLEM 6.5.1 A satellite is placed into an orbit about the earth. At injection (burnout of the carrier rocket) the speed of the satellite is v_0 and its altitude is y_0. Express the satellite's subsequent speed v as a function of its altitude y.

PROBLEM 6.5.2 The period T of the earth about the sun is one year. The distance from the earth to the sun at perihelion (closest approach) is 91.3×10^6 miles and at aphelion (farthest approach) is 93.5×10^6 miles. Determine the mass of the sun.

PROBLEM 6.5.3 An earth satellite is released at an altitude of 250 miles with a velocity of 5.5 miles/sec in the horizontal direction. Taking the radius of the earth as 4,000 miles, find the orbit height at apogee and perigee and calculate the period of the orbit.

PROBLEM 6.5.4 At its perihelion, Mars is about 128.8×10^6 miles from the sun, while at aphelion it is 154.8×10^6 miles from the sun. Find the period of the orbit of Mars.

PROBLEM 6.5.5 Find the time required for an earth satellite to traverse a circular orbit 520 miles above the earth.

PROBLEM 6.5.6 Find the horizontal velocity at which a satellite must be traveling to enter an elliptical orbit at 550 miles above the earth if the eccentricity of the orbit is to be $e = 0.9$.

Motion of a particle

An earth satellite moving in a circular orbit of radius r_1 is transferred to a circular orbit of radius $r_2 > r_1$ along a semiellipse tangent to the initial and to the final orbit. This so-called *Hohmann transfer* is effected by means of speed impulses (by rocket thrusts of negligibly short time) Δv_1 at the beginning and Δv_2 at the end of the transfer. Write expressions for these speed impulses in terms of r_1 and r_2. What should the maneuver be if a Hohmann transfer is desired for an orbit change for which $r_2 < r_1$?

PROBLEM 6.5.7

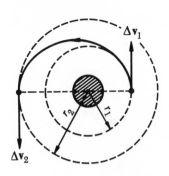

Observations of the orbit of a satellite reveal that its altitudes of closest and farthest approach (perigee and apogee) are 150 and 600 miles, respectively. Calculate the eccentricity and period of the orbit.

PROBLEM 6.5.8

At one instant of its motion an earth satellite is at an altitude of 400 miles and its velocity has a radial component of 2,000 mph and a transverse component of 16,000 mph. What is the orbital period?

PROBLEM 6.5.9

A manned satellite is in orbit about the earth. Its minimum altitude (perigee) is 200 miles, and its speed there is 18,500 mph. In order to decrease his closest approach to earth by 100 miles, the astronaut fires a short burst on his retro-rockets at perigee, decreasing his speed by Δv. Compute Δv.

PROBLEM 6.5.10

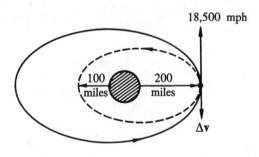

The ratios of the radii and gravitational accelerations of Mars and the earth are 0.532 and 0.385, respectively. What is the speed of a satellite in a circular orbit about Mars at an altitude of 200 miles above its surface?

PROBLEM 6.5.11

Planetary orbits

APPLICATIONS IN PLANE DYNAMICS: MOTION OF A RIGID BODY AND OF A SYSTEM

Section 7.1 Moments of inertia.
Kinetic energy and angular momentum

SAMPLE PROBLEM A homogeneous thin disk has mass m and thickness t. Find its moment of inertia about a diameter.

Solution

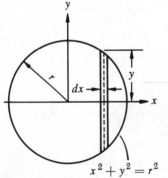

Consider the disk to be made of thin bars of width dx, length $l = 2y$, and thickness t. The mass of an elemental bar is $M = (2y\,dx/\pi r^2)m$. The moment of inertia of a bar about the x-axis is

$$\frac{1}{12}Ml^2 = \frac{1}{12}\frac{2y\,dx}{\pi r^2}m(2y)^2$$

But since $y = \sqrt{r^2 - x^2}$, and the total moment of inertia is the sum of the moments of inertia of the parts, we have

$$I = \frac{2m}{3\pi r^2}\int_{-r}^{r}(r^2 - x^2)^{3/2}\,dx$$

$$= \frac{2m}{3\pi r^2}\left\{\frac{x}{4}(r^2 - x^2)^{3/2} + \frac{3r^2 x}{8}\sqrt{r^2 - x^2}\right.$$

$$\left. + \frac{3r^4}{8}\sin^{-1}\frac{x}{r}\right\}\Big|_{-r}^{r}$$

so $$I = \frac{mr^2}{4}$$

116

CHAPTER 7

A homogeneous thin triangular plate is positioned with its side AB parallel to the x-axis and its vertices touching the axes as shown. Find the radius of gyration of plate ABC about the x-axis. The height OA of the triangle is h and the length of side AB is b.

PROBLEM 7.1.1

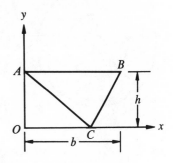

The homogeneous thin trapezoidal plate of mass m shown in the figure has two sides parallel to the x-axis. Side OC of length b is on the x-axis, and side AB of length a is at a distance h from the x-axis. Find the moment of inertia of the plate about the x-axis.

PROBLEM 7.1.2

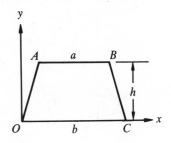

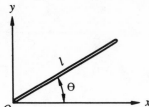

PROBLEM 7.1.3 A homogeneous slender rod of mass m and length l lies in the xy-plane inclined at an angle θ with respect to the x-axis. Find the moment of inertia of the rod about the x-axis.

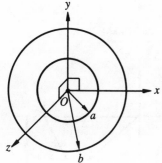

PROBLEM 7.1.4 A homogeneous thin ring of mass m, inner radius a, and outer radius b lies in the xy-plane.
(a) Find the moment of inertia about the z-axis.
(b) Find the moment of inertia about the x-axis.

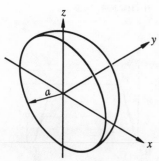

PROBLEM 7.1.5 Given a solid homogeneous hemisphere of mass m and radius a, calculate
(a) The moment of inertia about the x-axis;
(b) The moment of inertia about the y-axis.

Motion of a rigid body and of a system

A cylindrical shaft 10 in. long and 3 in. in diameter is made of a homogeneous material. A 1-in. diameter hole is drilled tangent to and parallel with the z-axis as shown. Find the radius of gyration about the z-axis.

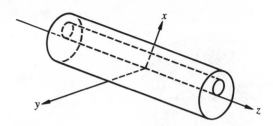

The L-shaped block shown in the figure is made of a homogeneous material weighing 0.3 lb/in.[3] Determine the moment of inertia of the block with respect to the x-, y-, and z-axes.

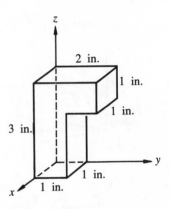

A homogeneous thin disk of mass m has the shape of a circular sector as shown. Find the moment of inertia about
(a) The x-axis;
(b) The y-axis.

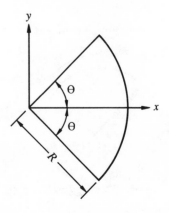

Moments of inertia. Kinetic energy, angular momentum   *119*

PROBLEM 7.1.9   A circular homogeneous thin disk of radius b, thickness t, and density ρ has a semicircular hole of radius a cut in it as shown. Find the moments of inertia about the x- and y-axes.

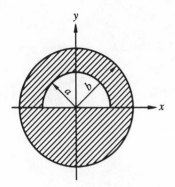

PROBLEM 7.1.10

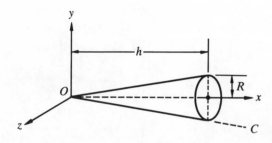

Determine the moments of inertia of the homogeneous right circular cone of mass m
(a) About the x-axis;
(b) About the y-axis;
(c) About the directrix OC.

PROBLEM 7.1.11   A homogeneous cylinder of radius 10 in. and weight 25 lb rolls without slipping on a planar surface. Its mass center moves in a straight line with a speed of 8 ft/sec. What is the kinetic energy of the cylinder? What is its angular momentum relative to the mass center?

PROBLEM 7.1.12   An unbalanced wheel rolls without slipping on a plane. Its geometric center O has a velocity of 5 ft/sec to the right. The wheel has a radius of 10 in. and weighs 30 lb. Its mass center G is at a radial distance of 2 in. from O as shown. The radius of gyration of the wheel about a perpendicular axis through G is 8 in. What is the angular momentum of the wheel relative to mass center G? What is the kinetic energy of the wheel when the mass center G is at its lowest point?

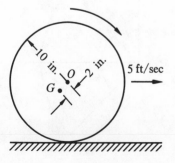

Motion of a rigid body and of a system

A uniform thin rod of weight W and length L is in contact with a horizontal floor and a vertical wall as shown. When the rod makes an angle θ with the horizontal, the velocity of the lower end is $\mathbf{v}$ to the left. Determine the kinetic energy of the rod. What is the angular momentum relative to the center of mass?

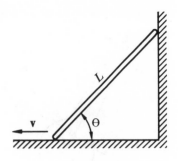

Section 7.2 Rigid body rotating about a fixed axis

The compound pendulum of mass m can rotate without friction about a fixed axis at O as shown. The pendulum's center of mass G is located a distance $\bar{r}$ from O, and its radius of gyration about the axis through O is k_0. If the pendulum is released from rest when it is horizontal ($\theta = 0$), find the bearing reaction at O as a function of the position of the pendulum.

SAMPLE PROBLEM

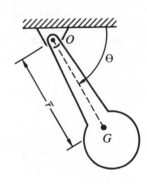

Solution

Taking normal and tangential components of

$$\Sigma \mathbf{F} = m\mathbf{a}$$

where $\mathbf{a}$ is the acceleration of G, we have

$$R_n - mg \sin \theta = m\bar{r}\dot{\theta}^2 \qquad mg \cos \theta - R_t = m\bar{r}\ddot{\theta} \qquad (1)$$

Thus we need expressions for $\dot{\theta}$ and $\ddot{\theta}$. Since only weight does work, the system is conservative; i.e., choosing potential energy zero at the horizontal rest position, we have

$$T + V = E = 0$$

so that

$$\tfrac{1}{2} mk_0^2 \dot{\theta}^2 - mg\bar{r} \cos \theta = 0$$

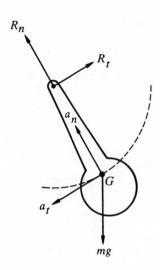

and
$$\dot{\theta}^2 = 2g\frac{\bar{r}}{k_0^2}\sin\theta \qquad (2)$$

To obtain an expression for $\ddot{\theta}$ we invoke the moment equation. Taking moments about the fixed axis through O we have

$$mg\bar{r}\cos\theta = mk_0^2\ddot{\theta}$$

whence
$$\ddot{\theta} = g\frac{\bar{r}}{k_0^2}\cos\theta \qquad (3)$$

Substituting (2) and (3) in (1) and solving for the components of the bearing reaction, we obtain

$$R_n = \left(1 + 2\frac{\bar{r}^2}{k_0^2}\right)mg\sin\theta \qquad R_t = \left(1 - \frac{\bar{r}^2}{k_0^2}\right)mg\cos\theta$$

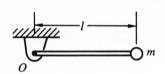

PROBLEM 7.2.1   The pendulum shown in the figure consists of a small mass m suspended at the end of a weightless rod of length l. The pendulum is released from rest in the horizontal position as shown. Calculate the reaction at the point of suspension O at the instant of release.

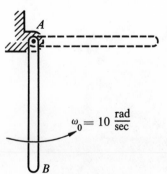

PROBLEM 7.2.2   A 2-ft-long uniform rod weighs 20 lb and is attached to a frictionless pivot at A. The rod is given an angular velocity of $\omega_0 = 10$ radians/sec counterclockwise when it is vertical, as shown. When the rod reaches a horizontal position, the attachment at A is released and the rod can then move freely. What is the maximum height above this horizontal position to which the center of gravity of the rod will rise?

Motion of a rigid body and of a system

A weightless cord is wrapped around the solid homogeneous 75-lb cylinder whose radius $r = 1$ ft. If the cylinder is released from rest, find the velocity of the mass center after it has descended a distance of 10 ft.

PROBLEM 7.2.3

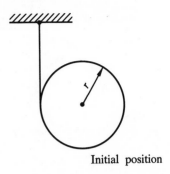

Initial position

The bar AB is held in a vertical position by the weightless cord BC as the system rotates with angular velocity ω about the vertical axis y-y. The pin at A is smooth and the bar AB weighs 32.2 lb. If the cord BC can support a maximum tension of 120 lb, find the limiting angular velocity of the system.

PROBLEM 7.2.4

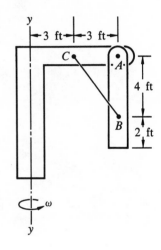

A homogeneous circular disk of mass M and radius R is free to rotate without friction about a fixed horizontal axis normal to its face and passing through its center O. A point mass m is attached to the edge of the disk. The disk is released from rest at the position shown ($\theta = \pi/2$). Find the angular velocity and acceleration of the system as a function of θ.

PROBLEM 7.2.5

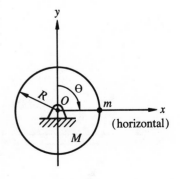

Rigid body rotating about a fixed axis

PROBLEM 7.2.6 A homogeneous semicircular disk of mass M and radius R is released from rest in the position shown. If no slipping occurs and $\phi_0 \ll 1$ (small oscillations), find the period of the oscillations.

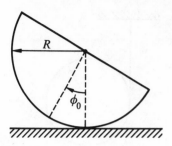

PROBLEM 7.2.7 A right circular cone of mass m rolls without slipping on a fixed conical surface such that the component of its angular velocity about the vertical axis is ω. Show that the kinetic energy of the cone is

$$T = \frac{9}{20} mh^2\omega^2 \left(1 + \frac{r^2}{6h^2} \right)$$

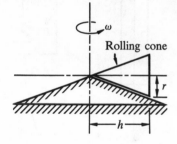

Rolling cone

PROBLEM 7.2.8 A uniform rod 5 ft long and of weight W is pinned smoothly at one end and allowed to rotate under the action of gravity in a vertical plane from a horizontal position of rest.
(a) Find the reactions at the point of support when it passes the 45° position and when it is in the vertical position.
(b) Find the kinetic energy of the rod in these positions.

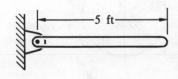

5 ft

Motion of a rigid body and of a system

A homogeneous door of mass M is acted on by a constant force F perpendicular to the door as shown, so that it turns through an angle of $90°$ in 2 sec. Find the magnitude of force F.

PROBLEM 7.2.9

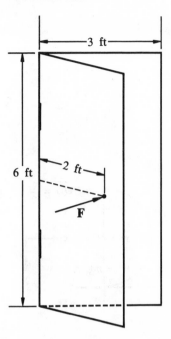

A flywheel with a moment of inertia of 5,000 lb-ft² about its central axis starts to rotate from rest. After 50 revolutions it has attained an angular speed of 70 rpm. Determine the constant torque acting on the flywheel.

PROBLEM 7.2.10

What constant torque acts on the flywheel of Prob. 7.2.10 in order that it accelerate from 10 to 80 rpm in 50 revolutions?

PROBLEM 7.2.11

Section 7.3 General motion of a rigid body parallel to a fixed plane

A thin uniform bar of weight W, bent into a semicircular shape of radius r, is released from rest in the position shown. If slipping does not take place, determine the initial acceleration $\mathbf{a}_0$ of the center O of the semicircle.

SAMPLE PROBLEM

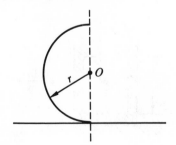

Solution

The equations of motion of the bar are

$$\Sigma \mathbf{F} = m\mathbf{a}_G$$

where $\mathbf{a}_G$ = acceleration of center of gravity G

$$\Sigma M = I_G \dot{\omega}$$

where I_G = moment of inertia about the axis through G perpendicular to the plane of the bar

$\dot{\omega}$ = angular acceleration of the bar

Since the bar is initially at rest, $\omega = 0$, and so

$$\mathbf{a}_G = \mathbf{a}_0 + \dot{\omega} \times \overrightarrow{OG}$$

where $a_0 = a_{0x} = r\dot{\omega}$ (no slip)

$$a_{0y} = 0$$

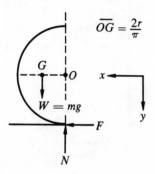

$\overline{OG} = \frac{2r}{\pi}$ Hence

$$\Sigma F_x = F = ma_{Gx} = ma_{0x} = ma_0 = mr\dot{\omega} \tag{1}$$

$$\Sigma F_y = W - N = ma_{Gy} = m\frac{2r}{\pi}\dot{\omega} \tag{2}$$

$$\Sigma M = \frac{2\pi}{r}N - Fr = I_G\dot{\omega} \tag{3}$$

Solving (1) to (3) for $\dot{\omega}$, F, and N, we get

$$a_0 = r\dot{\omega} = \frac{Wr\dfrac{2r}{\pi}}{I_G + mr^2 + m\left(\dfrac{2r}{\pi}\right)^2}$$

But by the parallel axis theorem

$$I_G = I_0 - m\left(\frac{2r}{\pi}\right)^2 = mr^2 - m\left(\frac{2r}{\pi}\right)^2$$

so that $$a_0 = \frac{2r^2}{\pi}\frac{W}{2mr^2} = \frac{g}{\pi}$$

PROBLEM 7.3.1 The 5-lb plunger is released from rest in the position shown where the linear spring is compressed to one-half its free length of 6 in. Determine the maximum velocity reached by the plunger in its subsequent upward motion. The spring is not attached to the plunger.

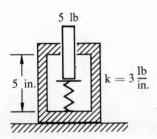

5 lb

5 in.

$k = 3\,\dfrac{\text{lb}}{\text{in.}}$

Motion of a rigid body and of a system

A uniform 10-ft pole weighing 50 lb is initially placed against a smooth vertical wall so that $\theta = 45°$. A constant 25-lb force acts against the bottom of the pole parallel to the smooth floor. Find the angular velocity of the pole after the lower end has moved 5 ft toward the wall.

PROBLEM 7.3.2

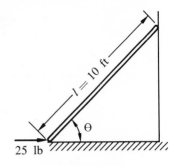

A homogeneous sphere of radius r and mass m rolls from rest down a plane inclined at angle ϕ to the horizontal. Find the velocity of its mass center after the sphere has been rolling for t sec. Assume that no slipping takes place.

PROBLEM 7.3.3

The homogeneous cylinder shown weighs 200 lb and rolls without slipping on the horizontal plane. The spring has a constant k of 40 lb/ft and its unstretched length is 3 ft. Find the angular velocity of the cylinder when it has moved 2 ft to the right of the position shown.

PROBLEM 7.3.4

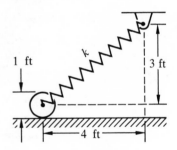

A uniform sphere of diameter d starts from rest on the top of a fixed sphere of diameter $D > d$ and rolls without slipping under the action of gravity.
(a) Find the angle θ at which the smaller sphere leaves the surface of the larger sphere.
(b) Find the corresponding angular velocity of the smaller sphere.

PROBLEM 7.3.5

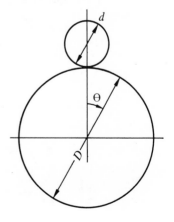

General motion of rigid body parallel to fixed plane   *127*

PROBLEM 7.3.6 A uniform slender rod of mass m and length l lies on a smooth horizontal plane and is initially at rest. Two forces, each of magnitude F, act on the rod as shown and remain perpendicular to the rod at all times. What is the acceleration of the center of gravity G? What is the acceleration of point C, which is halfway between G and A?

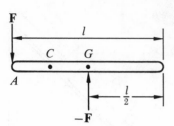

PROBLEM 7.3.7 An automobile weighing 2 tons rounds a curve of radius 150 ft at a speed of 60 mph. Determine the radial component of the friction force on the tires.

$v = 60$ mph

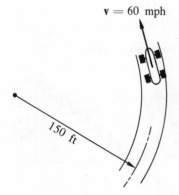

PROBLEM 7.3.8 The uniform 2-ft rod weighing 10 lb is attached to a small weightless roller and is free to rotate about the roller axis. The system is originally at rest, with the rod hanging in the vertical plane. A constant horizontal 5-lb force is suddenly applied to the upper end. Find the acceleration of the center of gravity of the rod and its angular acceleration.

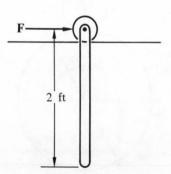

Motion of a rigid body and of a system

The uniform sphere shown has a diameter of 1 ft and weighs 32.2 lb. It rolls without slipping down a circular guide of 3-ft radius starting at the position $\theta = 90°$. Find the normal reaction on the sphere as it passes the bottom of the guide ($\theta = 0$).

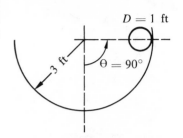

$D = 1$ ft

3 ft

$\theta = 90°$

Bar AB, pinned smoothly to light rollers, is constrained such that end A moves in a horizontal slot while connected to a linear spring, and end B moves in a vertical slot. The bar is 10 in. long and weighs 30 lb. The spring has an unstretched length of 8 in. and a spring constant $k = 3$ lb/in. If the bar is released from rest in the position shown, find its angular velocity and the linear velocity of the end B at the instant the bar passes through the horizontal position.

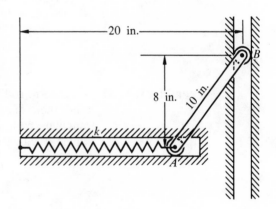

20 in.

8 in.

10 in.

k

B

A

The uniform rod AB is 2 ft long and weighs 10 lb. End A moves along a horizontal guide with a speed of 150 ft/sec. End B is pinned to crank OB of length 0.5 ft. At the instant shown, find
(a) The kinetic energy of rod AB;
(b) The angular momentum of rod AB with respect to its center of mass, to end A, and to end B.

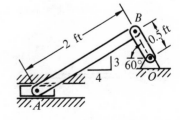

B

2 ft

0.5 ft

3

60°

4

A

O

General motion of rigid body parallel to fixed plane   129

PROBLEM 7.3.12 A uniform wheel of radius R and mass M has a rope wound around its axle of radius r. A horizontal force $\mathbf{F}$ is applied to the rope. If the wheel rolls without slipping, what is the acceleration of its center of mass?

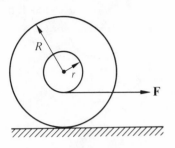

PROBLEM 7.3.13 A uniform rod of length $2l$ is balanced vertically on the floor, then displaced slightly and allowed to fall. Find its angular acceleration and angular velocity as a function of the angle θ with the vertical if the floor is so rough that the lower end cannot slip.

PROBLEM 7.3.14 A uniform rod of length $2l$ is balanced vertically on the floor and then displaced slightly and allowed to fall. Find its angular acceleration and angular velocity as a function of the angle θ with the vertical if the floor is smooth and slipping occurs.

PROBLEM 7.3.15 A sphere of radius r rolls without slipping on a larger sphere of radius R, starting from rest at the top. If ϕ is the angle between the line of centers and the vertical, find $\ddot{\phi}$ and $\dot{\phi}$ in terms of ϕ.

PROBLEM 7.3.16 The uniform rod of length $2l$ is supported in the horizontal position shown. End A is released and swings around end B until the rod is vertical, at which time end B is released.
(a) Find the trajectory of the center of gravity of the rod after B is released.
(b) What are the angular velocity and the angular acceleration of the rod after B is released?

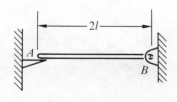

Motion of a rigid body and of a system

A uniform rod of length l and weight W is in contact with two smooth walls, one vertical and the other horizontal; the rod is at rest when inclination angle $\theta = \theta_0$.
(a) Write the equations of motion of the rod.
(b) Determine the angular velocity of the rod as a function of angular position θ.
(c) Find the angle θ at which the end A loses contact with the wall.

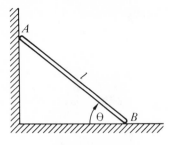

Section 7.4   Normal modes of vibration

The linear spring-mass system shown in the figure is governed by the differential equation of motion

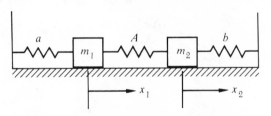

$$m_1\ddot{x}_1 + ax_1 + A(x_1 - x_2) = 0 \quad (1)$$

$$m_2\ddot{x}_2 + bx_2 - A(x_1 - x_2) = 0 \quad (2)$$

where m_1 and m_2 are the masses and a, b, and A are the spring constants.

Show that the roots C_i, $i = 1, 2$, of the quadratic equation

$$C^2 + \left(\frac{a}{A}R + R - \frac{b}{A} - 1\right)C - R = 0$$

where $\qquad R = \dfrac{m_2}{m_1}$

will allow the uncoupling of differential equations (1) and (2) into equations for normal modes by the substitution of $x_1 = C_i x_2$ into Eq. (1) or (2). Compare this method for finding normal modes with the method presented in the text (Synge and Griffith).

Normal modes of vibration

131

PROBLEM 7.4.2 Find the normal modes of the coupled system

$$\ddot{x}_1 + 2x_1 + (x_1 - x_2) = 0$$

$$2\ddot{x}_2 + 3x_2 - (x_1 - x_2) = 0$$

(a) By the method outlined in Prob. 7.4.1;

(b) By the method discussed in the text (Synge and Griffith).

PROBLEM 7.4.3 A uniform slender rod OC of length $2a$ and weight P is suspended from end O. A second uniform rod of length l and weight Q is attached at its center of mass to end C. Rod OC is inclined initially at a small angle ϕ_0 to the vertical, and rod AB has an initial angular speed $\dot{\theta}_0$, where θ is the angular position of the rod AB with respect to the vertical. Neglecting friction, show that the motion can be described approximately by the relations

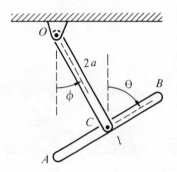

$$\phi = \phi_0 \cos\left[\left(\frac{3}{4}\frac{P + 2Q}{P + 3Q}\right)\frac{g}{a}\right]^{\frac{1}{2}} t$$

$$\theta = \dot{\theta}_0 t$$

PROBLEM 7.4.4 A pendulum composed of a bob of mass m at the end of a weightless rod of length l is attached to a block of mass M which slides on a horizontal surface and is attached to a fixed wall by a linear spring with constant k. Friction can be neglected. Show that the frequencies for small oscillations are governed by the equation

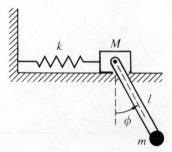

$$n^4 - \left(\frac{k}{n} + \frac{g}{l}\frac{M + m}{M}\right)n^2 + \frac{k}{M}\frac{g}{l} = 0$$

Motion of a rigid body and of a system

Determine the normal modes for small vibrations of the two coupled pendulums shown in the figure. The weightless rods are connected by a simple spring attached at a distance h from the support. Each bob has a mass m and the spring constant is k. If ϕ_1 and ϕ_2 are the coordinates of the motion, show that the kinetic energy of the system is

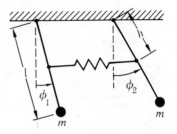

$$T = \tfrac{1}{2}ml^2 \left(\dot{\phi}_1{}^2 + \dot{\phi}_2{}^2 \right)$$

and that the potential energy can be approximated by

$$V \cong \tfrac{1}{2}mgl \left(\phi_1{}^2 + \phi_2{}^2 \right) + \tfrac{1}{2}kh^2 \left(\phi_2 - \phi_1 \right)^2$$

Show that the normal modes have frequencies

$$n_1 = \sqrt{\frac{g}{l}} \quad \text{and} \quad n_2 = \left(\frac{g}{l} + \frac{2kh^2}{ml^2} \right)^{1/2}$$

Determine the normal modes for the system of two masses and two simple springs constrained to move vertically. The weights are $W_1 = 10$ lb and $W_2 = 20$ lb, and the spring constants are $k_1 = 100$ lb/ft and $k_2 = 200$ lb/ft.

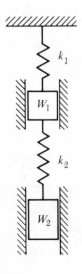

PROBLEM 7.4.7

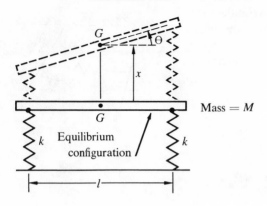

G

θ

x

G

Mass $= M$

k Equilibrium
       configuration

k

l

Using x, θ as the coordinates, set up the differential equation of motion and find the natural frequencies for small displacements of the system shown.

PROBLEM 7.4.8

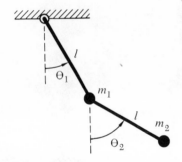

l

θ_1

m_1

l m_2

θ_2

Write the equations of motion for the double pendulum, assuming a small amplitude of the oscillations, and find the frequencies of the normal modes.

Section 7.5   Stability of equilibrium

PROBLEM 7.5.1

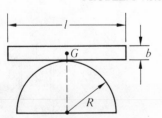

l

G

b

R

A uniform square beam of length l and thickness b is balanced on a semicircular cylinder of radius R as shown. Discuss stability of equilibrium of the beam.

Motion of a rigid body and of a system

Determine the equilibrium position of the uniform semi-circular cylinder of radius r resting on the rough plane inclined at angle α to the horizontal. The coefficient of friction is μ. Find the relation among the parameters of the system that will ensure stable equilibrium.

PROBLEM 7.5.2

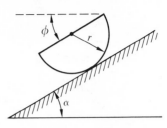

Investigate the possible equilibrium positions for a particle with the potential energy functions given below. Determine whether the equilibrium positions are stable.

PROBLEM 7.5.3

(a) $V(\theta) = 1 - \cos \theta$

(b) $V(x) = x^3 - x^2 - 4x + 4$

(c) $V(x) = x^4 - 3x^2 + 2$

A uniform half cylinder of radius r_1 rests on top of a fixed half cylinder of radius r_2 as shown in the figure. The surfaces are sufficiently rough to prevent slipping. Find the necessary relation between r_1 and r_2 in order that the given position be one of stable equilibrium.

PROBLEM 7.5.4

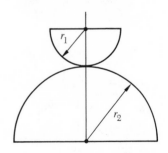

The uniform body shown in the figure rests on a horizontal plane. Find the relationship between h and r such that the position of the body is stable.

PROBLEM 7.5.5

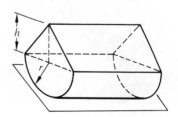

Stability of equilibrium

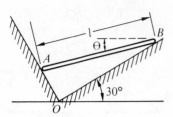

PROBLEM 7.5.6 A uniform rod AB of length l and weight W rests in a smooth-sided, right-angled trough. Side OB of the trough is inclined at 30° to the horizontal. Find the angle θ between the rod and the horizontal at equilibrium. Discuss the stability of equilibrium.

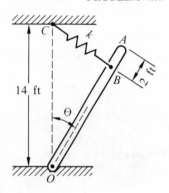

PROBLEM 7.5.7 The uniform bar OA of length 12 ft and weight 30 lb is pinned smoothly at O. The simple spring BC has a constant $k = 20$ lb/ft and an unstretched length of 5 ft. Find the equilibrium position θ and investigate its stability.

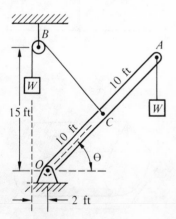

PROBLEM 7.5.8 Beam OA is 20 ft long and has negligible weight. It is pinned at O, carries a weight W at A, and is supported by another weight W as shown. Friction at pin O and pulley B is negligible. Determine the equilibrium position θ and discuss its stability.

Motion of a rigid body and of a system

PLANE IMPULSIVE MOTION

Section 8.1 General theory of plane impulsive motion

PROBLEM 8.1.1

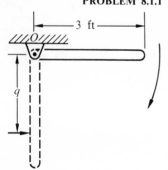

A thin uniform bar of length 3 ft and weight 10 lb swings in a vertical plane about a horizontal axis passing through one end of the bar. As the bar reaches the vertical position, it hits a stop located at a distance q below the point of suspension. What is the distance q so that the impact causes no reaction at the point of suspension?

PROBLEM 8.1.2

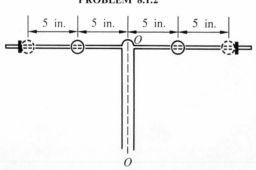

The light, smooth rod shown supports two sliding balls of negligible dimensions. The balls weigh 4 lb each. The system is rotating about the vertical at 25 radians/sec when the balls are released from their initial position 5 in. from the vertical center line O–O.

(a) Find the angular velocity of the rod when the balls have moved out to 10 in. from the center. Assuming no friction, has there been any change in kinetic energy?

CHAPTER 8

(b) What is the radial velocity of the balls in the 10-in. position?

(c) Suppose the balls hit stops located at the 10-in. position and are locked in place there. Determine the angular velocity of the rod after impact and the change in kinetic energy of the system.

A 100-lb block falls to the ground from a height of 15 ft. What is the magnitude of the impulse on the block during the time interval it is brought to rest? If this time interval is 0.05 sec, what is the average magnitude of the force exerted on the block by the ground? **PROBLEM 8.1.3**

A bullet of weight 0.025 lb is fired from a 25-lb rifle and attains a muzzle speed of 1,200 ft/sec. What is the speed of the recoiling rifle? **PROBLEM 8.1.4**

A thin plate is at rest on a smooth table. It is struck an impulsive blow parallel to the table at point A. If the impulse is $\hat{\mathbf{F}}$ and the velocity of point A after the blow is $\mathbf{v}$, what is the kinetic energy of the plate after the blow? **PROBLEM 8.1.5**

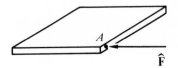

Section 8.2   Collisions

A tennis ball strikes the court with a velocity **v** making an angle θ with the vertical. If the coefficient of restitution is e and the coefficient of friction between the ball and court is negligibly small, what is the velocity of rebound **v'**?

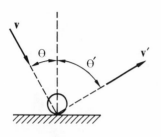

Solution

From conservation of momentum parallel to the ground,

$$v \sin \theta = v' \sin \theta' \qquad (1)$$

By hypothesis

$$v_s = ev_a$$

where $\quad v_a = v \cos \theta - V \qquad v_s = V' - (-v' \cos \theta')$

and the speed of the ground $V = V' = 0$.

Hence

$$ev \cos \theta = v' \cos \theta' \qquad (2)$$

From Eqs. (1) and (2) we get

$$v' = v \sqrt{e^2 \cos^2 \theta + \sin^2 \theta}$$

$$\tan \theta' = \frac{1}{e} \tan \theta$$

A number of identical spheres are placed in a line on a smooth table. Sphere 1 strikes sphere 2 with an initial speed V, and sphere 2 then strikes sphere 3, etc., all along the same line. If the coefficient of restitution is e, show that the speed of the nth sphere after impact is

$$V_n = (1 + e)^{n-1} \frac{V}{2^{n-1}}$$

Two uniform, smooth, perfectly elastic spheres collide with initial velocities of the same magnitude v. The left sphere has an initial velocity in the direction of the line of centers of the spheres, and the velocity of the right sphere has a direction inclined at an angle θ with the line of centers as shown. Find the velocities of the spheres after impact. $|\mathbf{v}_1| = |\mathbf{v}_2| = v$.

PROBLEM 8.2.2

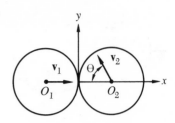

A steel bearing falls from a height h and bounces vertically and continuously until motion ceases. If the coefficient of restitution is e, show that the distance traversed by the bearing is

$$\frac{1 + e^2}{1 - e^2} h$$

PROBLEM 8.2.3

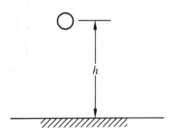

A particle with initial speed v_0 strikes a particle of the same mass initially at rest. If half the original kinetic energy is lost, find the velocities of the two particles after the collision.

PROBLEM 8.2.4

A tennis ball initially at rest falls freely from a height of 200 ft. After striking the ground, it bounces to a height of 160 ft. Determine the coefficient of restitution and the loss of energy.

PROBLEM 8.2.5

A particle of mass m strikes and becomes attached to a particle of mass M which is originally at rest. Determine the fraction of the kinetic energy lost.

PROBLEM 8.2.6

A tennis ball hits a horizontal plane at an angle of 30°. If the speed of the ball is 25 ft/sec and the coefficient of restitution is 0.8, find the direction and magnitude of the rebound velocity. Neglect tangential friction.

PROBLEM 8.2.7

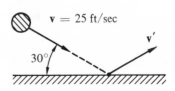

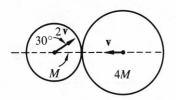

PROBLEM 8.2.8 Two smooth spheres collide as shown. If the coefficient of restitution is 0.9, find the velocity of each sphere after impact.

Section 8.3   Applications

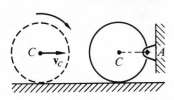

SAMPLE PROBLEM A uniform circular disk of mass m and radius r rolls without slipping on a plane surface so that its center of mass C has a velocity v_c. Point A on the rim of the disk is suddenly fixed as shown. Determine the new velocity of the mass center v'_c.

Solution

The angular momentum relative to the perpendicular axis through fixed point A is

$$h = I_c \omega + m(x_c \dot{y}_c - y_c \dot{x}_c)$$

where $I_c = \frac{1}{2} mr^2$ = centroidal moment of inertia

ω = angular speed

At the beginning of impact:

$$\dot{x}_c = v_c = r\omega$$

$$\dot{y}_c = 0$$

$$y_c = 0$$

At the end of impact:

$$\dot{x}_c = 0$$

$$\dot{y}_c = r\omega' = v'_c$$

$$x_c = r$$

The impulsive force acts through A. All other forces are negligible by comparison; hence

$$\frac{1}{2} mr^2 \frac{v_c}{r} + 0 = \frac{1}{2} mr^2 \frac{v'_c}{r} + mrv'_c$$

so that $\qquad\qquad v'_c = \frac{1}{3} v_c$

142

Plane impulsive motion

The uniform rods AB and BC each of length $2l$ and mass m are smoothly hinged at B and placed on a smooth horizontal plane with AB perpendicular to BC as shown in the figure. An impulse force $\hat{\mathbf{F}}$ strikes rod AB at A in the direction of BC. Describe the resulting motion by finding the velocities of the centers of mass of each rod, their angular velocities, and the impulsive reaction at B.

PROBLEM 8.3.1

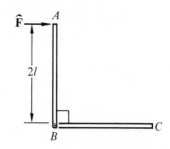

Find the energy lost by a locomotive of weight W whose speed before coupling is v, when it picks up a string of cars of weight w which are initially standing still.

PROBLEM 8.3.2

A ballistic pendulum is constructed by suspending a heavy box of sand from a rope 6 ft long. If a bullet is fired into the sand, the box will swing through some angle which can be measured to determine the initial velocity of the bullet. If a 1-oz bullet causes a 50-lb box to swing through an angle of 10°, find the initial velocity of the bullet.

PROBLEM 8.3.3

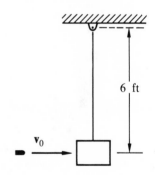

A wheel of radius R and mass M rolling on a horizontal surface strikes a step with a centroidal velocity $\mathbf{v}_0$. What is the maximum height h of the step if the wheel is able to roll over it?

PROBLEM 8.3.4

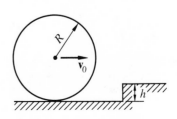

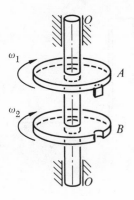

PROBLEM 8.3.5 Two sliding disks A and B are mounted on a stationary frictionless shaft as shown. Their centroidal moments of inertia about the shaft axis O–O are I_1 and I_2, respectively. Their angular speeds are ω_1 and ω_2, respectively. If they are suddenly locked together, what is the angular velocity of the coupled system?

PROBLEM 8.3.6 A uniform square plate of mass M and side l rests on a smooth horizontal table. A horizontal impulsive force of magnitude $\hat{F}$ is applied at a corner in a direction perpendicular to one of its edges. Find the subsequent motion of the plate.

PRODUCTS OF VECTORS

Section 9.1 The scalar and vector products

SAMPLE PROBLEM Find the unit vector along vectors $\vec{AB}$ and $\vec{AC}$, respectively. Find the unit vector perpendicular to the plane containing A, B, and C.

Solution

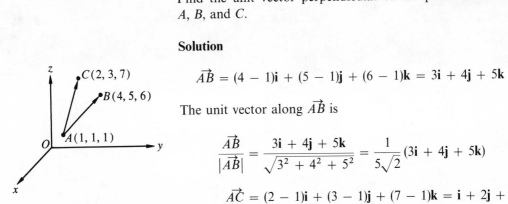

$$\vec{AB} = (4 - 1)\mathbf{i} + (5 - 1)\mathbf{j} + (6 - 1)\mathbf{k} = 3\mathbf{i} + 4\mathbf{j} + 5\mathbf{k}$$

The unit vector along $\vec{AB}$ is

$$\frac{\vec{AB}}{|\vec{AB}|} = \frac{3\mathbf{i} + 4\mathbf{j} + 5\mathbf{k}}{\sqrt{3^2 + 4^2 + 5^2}} = \frac{1}{5\sqrt{2}}(3\mathbf{i} + 4\mathbf{j} + 5\mathbf{k})$$

$$\vec{AC} = (2 - 1)\mathbf{i} + (3 - 1)\mathbf{j} + (7 - 1)\mathbf{k} = \mathbf{i} + 2\mathbf{j} + 6\mathbf{k}$$

The unit vector along $\vec{AC}$ is

$$\frac{\vec{AC}}{|\vec{AC}|} = \frac{\mathbf{i} + 2\mathbf{j} + 6\mathbf{k}}{\sqrt{1 + 4 + 36}} = \frac{1}{\sqrt{41}}(\mathbf{i} + 2\mathbf{j} + 6\mathbf{k})$$

$$\vec{AB} \times \vec{AC} = \begin{vmatrix} \mathbf{i} & \mathbf{j} & \mathbf{k} \\ 3 & 4 & 5 \\ 1 & 2 & 6 \end{vmatrix} = 14\mathbf{i} - 13\mathbf{j} + 2\mathbf{k}$$

CHAPTER 9

The unit vector perpendicular to $\vec{AC}$ and $\vec{AB}$ is

$$\frac{\vec{AB} \times \vec{AC}}{|\vec{AB} \times \vec{AC}|} = \frac{14\mathbf{i} - 13\mathbf{j} + 2\mathbf{k}}{\sqrt{14^2 + 13^2 + 2^2}} = \frac{1}{\sqrt{369}}(14\mathbf{i} - 13\mathbf{j} + 2\mathbf{k})$$

or
$$\frac{-1}{\sqrt{369}}(14\mathbf{i} - 13\mathbf{j} + 2\mathbf{k})$$

Find the vector projection of **B** onto **A** if $\mathbf{A} = 2\mathbf{i} + 3\mathbf{j} - \mathbf{k}$ and $\mathbf{B} = 3\mathbf{i} - \mathbf{j} + 2\mathbf{k}$. **PROBLEM 9.1.1**

Given vectors $\mathbf{A}(a_1,a_2,a_3)$ and $\mathbf{B}(b_1,b_2,b_3)$, find the magnitude and direction cosines of vector $\mathbf{C} = \mathbf{B} - \mathbf{A}$. **PROBLEM 9.1.2**

Evaluate the moment **M** about the origin of a 10-lb force which has direction cosines proportional to (3,4,5) and which acts at a point $A(1,2,3)$. **PROBLEM 9.1.3**

Do the following vectors **A**, **B**, and **C** form a right-handed triad? **PROBLEM 9.1.4**

$$\mathbf{A} = 2\mathbf{i} - \mathbf{j} + \mathbf{k} \qquad \mathbf{B} = -\mathbf{i} + 2\mathbf{j} + 2\mathbf{k} \qquad \mathbf{C} = \mathbf{i} + \mathbf{j} - \mathbf{k}$$

PROBLEM 9.1.5 Choose x, y, and z such that $\mathbf{i} + \mathbf{j} + 2\mathbf{k}$, $-\mathbf{i} + z\mathbf{k}$, and $2\mathbf{i} + x\mathbf{j} + y\mathbf{k}$ are mutually orthogonal.

PROBLEM 9.1.6 If $\mathbf{v} = \omega \times \mathbf{R}$, where $\omega = t\mathbf{i} + t^2\mathbf{j} + 3\mathbf{k}$ and $\mathbf{R} = 3t\mathbf{i} + t^3\mathbf{j} + t^5\mathbf{k}$, find $d\mathbf{v}/dt$.

PROBLEM 9.1.7 For any vector $\mathbf{R}$, prove that

$$\frac{d}{dt}\left(\mathbf{R} \times \frac{d\mathbf{R}}{dt}\right) = \mathbf{R} \times \frac{d^2\mathbf{R}}{dt^2}$$

PROBLEM 9.1.8 Find the unit vector which is perpendicular to both $3\mathbf{i} - 2\mathbf{j} + \mathbf{k}$ and $\mathbf{i} + \mathbf{j} - 2\mathbf{k}$.

Section 9.2 Triple products

SAMPLE PROBLEM Find the equation of the plane containing points $A(1,1,1)$, $B(4,5,6)$, and $C(2,3,7)$.

Solution

$$\vec{AB} = (4 - 1)\mathbf{i} + (5 - 1)\mathbf{j} + (6 - 1)\mathbf{k} = 3\mathbf{i} + 4\mathbf{j} + 5\mathbf{k}$$

$$\vec{AC} = \mathbf{i} + 2\mathbf{j} + 6\mathbf{k}$$

$$\vec{AB} \times \vec{AC} = 14\mathbf{i} - 13\mathbf{j} + 2\mathbf{k} = \mathbf{N} \qquad \text{(normal to the plane)}$$

Take any point $P(x,y,z)$ in the plane; $\vec{AP} \cdot \mathbf{N} = 0$

$$[(x - 1)\mathbf{i} + (y - 1)\mathbf{j} + (z - 1)\mathbf{k}] \cdot (14\mathbf{i} - 13\mathbf{j} + 2\mathbf{k}) = 0$$

$$14(x - 1) - 13(y - 1) + 2(z - 1) = 0$$

$$14x - 13y + 2z - 3 = 0$$

Prove that $\mathbf{A} \times (\mathbf{B} \times \mathbf{C}) + \mathbf{B} \times (\mathbf{C} \times \mathbf{A}) + \mathbf{C} \times (\mathbf{A} \times \mathbf{B})$ **PROBLEM 9.2.1**
$= 0$ for any three vectors $\mathbf{A}$, $\mathbf{B}$, and $\mathbf{C}$.

If $\mathbf{A} = \mathbf{i} + \mathbf{j} - \mathbf{k}$, $\mathbf{B} = 2\mathbf{i} + \mathbf{j} + \mathbf{k}$, and $\mathbf{C} = -\mathbf{i} - 2\mathbf{j} + 3\mathbf{k}$, **PROBLEM 9.2.2**
find
(a) $\mathbf{A} \times (\mathbf{B} \times \mathbf{C})$
(b) $\mathbf{A} \cdot (\mathbf{B} \times \mathbf{C})$
(c) $\mathbf{B} \cdot (\mathbf{A} \times \mathbf{C})$.

Show that **PROBLEM 9.2.3**

$$(\mathbf{A} \times \mathbf{B}) \cdot (\mathbf{C} \times \mathbf{D}) = \begin{vmatrix} \mathbf{A} \cdot \mathbf{C} & \mathbf{B} \cdot \mathbf{C} \\ \mathbf{A} \cdot \mathbf{D} & \mathbf{B} \cdot \mathbf{D} \end{vmatrix}$$

Given $\mathbf{A} = 2t^2\mathbf{i} + 5t\mathbf{j} - 8\mathbf{k}$ and $\mathbf{B} = 3\mathbf{i} + 6\mathbf{j}$, find $\dfrac{d}{dt}(\mathbf{B} \cdot \mathbf{A})$ **PROBLEM 9.2.4**
and $\dfrac{d}{dt}(\mathbf{B} \times \mathbf{A})$.

Integrate $\mathbf{A} \times \mathbf{B}$ with respect to time where $\mathbf{A} = 5t\mathbf{i} - (4t^3$ **PROBLEM 9.2.5**
$+ 6)\mathbf{j}$ and $\mathbf{B} = (-6t^2\mathbf{i} + 12\mathbf{k})$.

Integrate the vector $\mathbf{A} = (10 + 12t^2)\mathbf{j} + 8\mathbf{k}$ from time $t = 3$ **PROBLEM 9.2.6**
sec to time $t = 10$ sec.

Find the equation of the line which is parallel to the vector **PROBLEM 9.2.7**
$\mathbf{R} = 2\mathbf{i} + 3\mathbf{j} + 5\mathbf{k}$ and passes through the point $Q(3,4,5)$.

Find the equation of the plane which is normal to the vector **PROBLEM 9.2.8**
$\mathbf{N} = 14\mathbf{i} - 13\mathbf{j} + 2\mathbf{k}$ and contains the origin.

Triple products

Section 9.3 Moments of vectors

SAMPLE PROBLEM Find the moment of the vector $\mathbf{F} = 5\mathbf{i} + \mathbf{j} + \mathbf{k}$ acting at the origin about the line AB as shown.

Solution

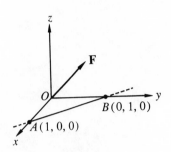

$$\vec{AO} = (-1)\mathbf{i}$$

$$\vec{AB} = (-1)\mathbf{i} + 1\mathbf{j} = -\mathbf{i} + \mathbf{j}$$

$$\frac{\vec{AB}}{|\vec{AB}|} = \frac{-\mathbf{i} + \mathbf{j}}{\sqrt{2}}$$

The moment of $\mathbf{F}$ about A is

$$\mathbf{G}_A = \vec{AO} \times \mathbf{F} = (-\mathbf{i}) \times (5\mathbf{i} + \mathbf{j} + \mathbf{k}) = -\mathbf{k} + \mathbf{j}$$

The moment of $\mathbf{F}$ about $\vec{AB}$ is

$$\mathbf{G}_A \cdot \frac{\vec{AB}}{|\vec{AB}|} = (-\mathbf{k} + \mathbf{j}) \cdot \frac{-\mathbf{i} + \mathbf{j}}{\sqrt{2}} = \frac{1}{\sqrt{2}}$$

PROBLEM 9.3.1 What is the moment about the point $(1,1,1)$ of the vector $4\mathbf{i} - 2\mathbf{j} + \mathbf{k}$ having its origin at the point $(1,3,5)$?

PROBLEM 9.3.2 Prove the following: If $\mathbf{A} + \mathbf{B} + \mathbf{C} = 0$, then $\mathbf{A} \times \mathbf{B} = \mathbf{B} \times \mathbf{C} = \mathbf{C} \times \mathbf{A}$. Is the converse true?

PROBLEM 9.3.3 What is the moment about the line $x = y = z$ of the vector $3\mathbf{i} + \mathbf{j} - 2\mathbf{k}$ acting at the point $(5,3,1)$?

PROBLEM 9.3.4 Find the moment of the vector $\mathbf{F} = 3\mathbf{i} + \mathbf{j}$ about the line AB as shown.

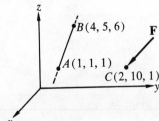

STATICS IN SPACE

Section 10.1   General force systems

SAMPLE PROBLEM

What is the moment of the force **F** about the origin and about the line AB?

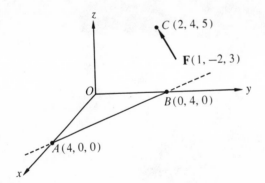

Solution

$$G_O = r_O \times F = \begin{vmatrix} \mathbf{i} & \mathbf{j} & \mathbf{k} \\ 2 & 4 & 5 \\ 1 & -2 & 3 \end{vmatrix} = 22\mathbf{i} - \mathbf{j} - 8\mathbf{k}$$

$$\mathbf{G}_A = \mathbf{r}_A \times \mathbf{F} = \begin{vmatrix} \mathbf{i} & \mathbf{j} & \mathbf{k} \\ (2-4) & 4 & 5 \\ 1 & -2 & 3 \end{vmatrix} = 22\mathbf{i} + 11\mathbf{j}$$

$$\vec{AB} = 4\mathbf{i} + 4\mathbf{j} \qquad \frac{\vec{AB}}{|\vec{AB}|} = \frac{\mathbf{i} + \mathbf{j}}{\sqrt{2}}$$

$$G_{AB} = \frac{\vec{AB}}{|\vec{AB}|} \cdot \mathbf{G}_A = \frac{1}{\sqrt{2}}(\mathbf{i} + \mathbf{j}) \cdot (22\mathbf{i} + 11\mathbf{j}) = \frac{33}{\sqrt{2}}$$

A force with components $(-2, -3, 8)$ acts at the point $(1,5,3)$. Find its moment about the origin and the moment about the line $x = y = z$; the positive sense of the line is in the direction of increasing x. **PROBLEM 10.1.1**

Two particles with position vectors $\mathbf{r}_1 = (\mathbf{i} + 2\mathbf{j} + 3\mathbf{k})$ and $\mathbf{r}_2 = (2\mathbf{i} + 4\mathbf{j} + 6\mathbf{k})$, respectively, are subjected to forces $\mathbf{P}_1 = (3\mathbf{i} + 4\mathbf{j} + 5\mathbf{k})$ and $\mathbf{P}_2 = 4(\mathbf{i} - 3\mathbf{j} + \mathbf{k})$, respectively. (a) Find the total force $\mathbf{F}$ and the total moment $\mathbf{G}$, taking the origin as base point. (b) Find the total force $\mathbf{F}'$ and total moment $\mathbf{G}'$ if the base point is moved to $(1,2,6)$. **PROBLEM 10.1.2**

PROBLEM 10.1.3 What are the scalar components of the total force and total moment if a system of particles having position vectors $\mathbf{R}_1 = 36\mathbf{i} + 4\mathbf{k}$, $\mathbf{R}_2 = 5\mathbf{i} + 3\mathbf{j} + \mathbf{k}$, and $\mathbf{R}_3 = \mathbf{j} + 3\mathbf{k}$ is acted upon by forces $\mathbf{P}_1 = 4\mathbf{k}$, $\mathbf{P}_2 = 3\mathbf{i} - 8\mathbf{j} - 2\mathbf{k}$, and $\mathbf{P}_3 = \mathbf{j} - \mathbf{k}$, where force $\mathbf{P}_i$ acts on the particle having position vector $\mathbf{R}_i$, and $i = 1,2,3$?

PROBLEM 10.1.4

The weightless curved bar shown is subjected to two arbitrary forces at ends A and B. What are the conditions for equilibrium?

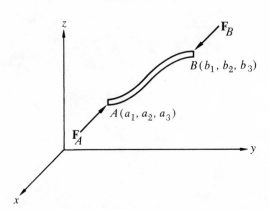

Section 10.2   Equilibrium of a system of particles

SAMPLE PROBLEM The equation of a space curve is written parametrically as $x = \cos t$, $y = \sin t$, and $c = t$. Find the tangential, normal, and binormal unit vectors at $t = 0$.

Solution

$$\mathbf{R} = x\mathbf{i} + y\mathbf{j} + c\mathbf{k} = \cos t\,\mathbf{i} + \sin t\,\mathbf{j} + t\mathbf{k}$$

$$\mathbf{t} = \frac{d\mathbf{R}}{|d\mathbf{R}|} = \frac{(-\sin t\,\mathbf{i} + \cos t\,\mathbf{j} + \mathbf{k})}{\sqrt{\sin^2 t + \cos^2 t + 1}}$$

$$= \frac{1}{\sqrt{2}}(-\sin t\,\mathbf{i} + \cos t\,\mathbf{j} + \mathbf{k})$$

At $t = 0$, $\qquad\qquad \mathbf{t} = (\mathbf{j} + \mathbf{k})\dfrac{1}{\sqrt{2}}$

Statics in space

$$\mathbf{n} = \frac{d\mathbf{t}}{|d\mathbf{t}|} = \frac{-\cos t\,\mathbf{i} - \sin t\,\mathbf{j}}{\sqrt{\cos^2 t + \sin^2 t}} = -\cos t\,\mathbf{i} - \sin t\,\mathbf{j}$$

At $t = 0$, $\qquad\qquad\qquad\qquad \mathbf{n} = -\mathbf{i}$

$$\mathbf{b} = \mathbf{t} \times \mathbf{n} = \frac{\mathbf{j} + \mathbf{k}}{\sqrt{2}} \times (-\mathbf{i}) = \frac{\mathbf{k} - \mathbf{j}}{\sqrt{2}} \qquad \text{at } t = 0$$

A ball weighing 10 lb is suspended from the joint of three weightless cables. The joint is located at (0,0,0); the other ends of the cables are fixed at points (2,5,5), (−5,2,5), and (−5,−2,5). Find the tension in the cables. **PROBLEM 10.2.1**

Specify the number and type (moment or force) of independent scalar equations which may be written for each of the following force systems in equilibrium: **PROBLEM 10.2.2**
(a) A general three-dimensional force system;
(b) A general concurrent system;
(c) A general coplanar system;
(d) A general parallel system;
(e) A coplanar parallel system;
(f) A concurrent coplanar system;
(g) A collinear system.

Prove the theorem: If a system of three forces $\mathbf{F}_1$, $\mathbf{F}_2$, and $\mathbf{F}_3$ is equipollent to zero, the system must be coplanar and either concurrent or parallel. **PROBLEM 10.2.3**

A cable is tightened around the edge of a plate as shown. Assuming that the tension in the cable is uniform and equal to T, find the force per unit length exerted on the edge of the plate by the cable. **PROBLEM 10.2.4**

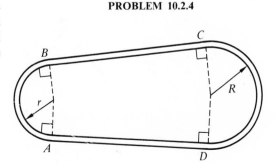

PROBLEM 10.2.5 Find the equation of the osculating plane to the space curve $x = t^2$, $y = t^3$, $z = t^4$ at the point $P_0(x_0, y_0, z_0)$, where $t = t_0$.

PROBLEM 10.2.6 Find the unit-principal normal vector, the radius of curvature, and the unit binormal vector for the curve which is represented parametrically by $x = 6 \sin 2t$, $y = 6 \cos 2t$, $z = 5t$.

PROBLEM 10.2.7 Find the radius of torsion τ for the space curve $x = e^t \cos t$, $y = e^t \sin t$, $z = e^t$.

PROBLEM 10.2.8

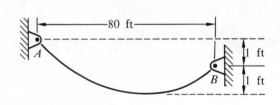

A cable weighing 40 lb is attached to supports A and B. Assuming that the weight is distributed uniformly along the horizontal, find the reaction forces at A and B.

PROBLEM 10.2.9

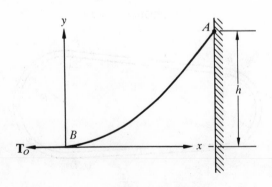

One end of a cable weighing ω lb/ft is attached to a wall at A. A horizontal force T_0 is applied at B as shown. Find the equation of the curve formed by the cable and determine the reaction at A.

Statics in space

Section 10.3 Reduction of force systems

Find the resultant force and resultant moment about points (0,0,0) ft and (1,2,5) ft, respectively, of the force system and couple shown.

Solution

$$\mathbf{F} = \Sigma \mathbf{F}_i = (-3)\mathbf{i} + (-2 + 2)\mathbf{j} + (1 + 4)\mathbf{k} = (-3\mathbf{i} + 5\mathbf{k}) \text{ lb}$$

The moment about (0,0,0) is

$$\mathbf{G}_0 = \Sigma \mathbf{r}_i \times \mathbf{F}_i + \mathbf{C}$$

$$= \begin{vmatrix} \mathbf{i} & \mathbf{j} & \mathbf{k} \\ 2 & 4 & 3 \\ -3 & 2 & 1 \end{vmatrix} + \begin{vmatrix} \mathbf{i} & \mathbf{j} & \mathbf{k} \\ 2 & 0 & 3 \\ 0 & -2 & 4 \end{vmatrix} + 6\mathbf{i} + \mathbf{j}$$

$$= (4 - 6 + 6)\mathbf{i} + (-9 - 2 - 8)\mathbf{j} + (4 + 12 - 4)\mathbf{k}$$

$$+ 6\mathbf{i} + \mathbf{j}$$

$$= 10\mathbf{i} - 18\mathbf{j} + 12\mathbf{k} \text{ ft-lb}$$

The moment about (1,2,5) is

$$\mathbf{G} = \Sigma \mathbf{r}_i \times \mathbf{F}_i + \mathbf{C} = \begin{vmatrix} \mathbf{i} & \mathbf{j} & \mathbf{k} \\ (2-1) & (4-2) & (3-5) \\ -3 & 2 & 1 \end{vmatrix}$$

$$+ \begin{vmatrix} \mathbf{i} & \mathbf{j} & \mathbf{k} \\ (2-1) & (-2) & (3-5) \\ 0 & -2 & 4 \end{vmatrix} + 6\mathbf{i} + \mathbf{j}$$

$$= (2 + 4 - 8 - 4)\mathbf{i} + (6 - 1 - 4)\mathbf{j} + (2 + 6 + 2)\mathbf{k}$$

$$+ 6\mathbf{i} + \mathbf{j}$$

$$= 0\mathbf{i} + 2\mathbf{j} + 10\mathbf{k} \text{ ft-lb}$$

Reduction of force systems

PROBLEM 10.3.1

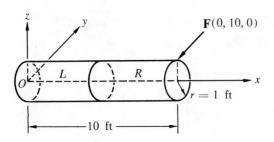

A uniform beam is fixed at one end with a force acting at the other end as shown. Find the forces across any section exerted by segment R on segment L.

PROBLEM 10.3.2

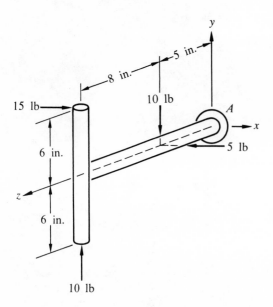

Find the reactions at A which result from the force system shown.

PROBLEM 10.3.3 Forces $\mathbf{F}_1 = (2\mathbf{i} + 3\mathbf{j} - 5\mathbf{k})$, $\mathbf{F}_2 = (\mathbf{i} - \mathbf{j} + \mathbf{k})$, and $\mathbf{F}_3 = (3\mathbf{i} + \mathbf{j})$ act at points $(1,2,3)$, $(-1,-2,-5)$, and $(2,-1,3)$, respectively. Reduce the system to a single force at the origin and a couple.

What are the necessary and sufficient conditions for a force system to be reducible to a single force?

PROBLEM 10.3.4

A 12-ft beam is subjected to the forces shown. Reduce the system of forces to a force at A and a couple. Reduce the given system to a single force.

PROBLEM 10.3.5

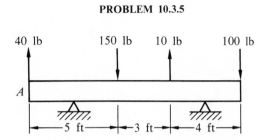

If the total force $\mathbf{F}$ and the total moment $\mathbf{G}$ for a given system are $\mathbf{F} = 7\mathbf{i} + 3\mathbf{j} + 4\mathbf{k}$ at $(1,3,5)$ and $\mathbf{G} = 4\mathbf{i} - 3\mathbf{k}$, find the equivalent wrench and the points of intersection of the axis of the wrench with the coordinate planes.

PROBLEM 10.3.6

Replace the forces shown by an equivalent force acting at point A, and determine the corresponding couple which must be applied.

PROBLEM 10.3.7

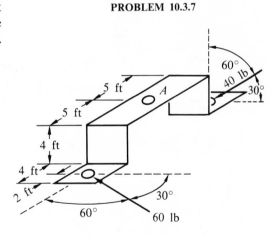

Prove that for any force system the product $\mathbf{F} \cdot \mathbf{G}$ is an invariant, where $\mathbf{F}$ is the resulting force and $\mathbf{G}$ is the resulting moment. Prove that $\mathbf{G}$ is least when the system is reduced to a wrench.

PROBLEM 10.3.8

PROBLEM 10.3.9 Forces $\mathbf{F}_1 = 3\mathbf{i} + 2\mathbf{j} - \mathbf{k}$ and $\mathbf{F}_2 = \mathbf{i} - 3\mathbf{j} + \mathbf{k}$ act at points $(1,2,3)$ and $(-1,3,5)$, respectively. If the system is to be reduced to a wrench, find the position vector of the new base point and the pitch of the wrench.

PROBLEM 10.3.10 A force $\mathbf{P}$ of magnitude $P = 10$ lb has direction cosines proportional to $(3,4,5)$ and acts at point $(1,2,3)$. Another force is equal to $-\mathbf{P}$ and acts at point $(-2,-3,-5)$. Find the vector moment of the couple resulting from both forces.

PROBLEM 10.3.11 Forces $\mathbf{F}_1 = (2\mathbf{i} + 3\mathbf{j} + \mathbf{k})$, $\mathbf{F}_2 = (-2\mathbf{i} - 3\mathbf{j} + \mathbf{k})$, and $\mathbf{F}_3 = (0 + 0 - 2\mathbf{k})$ act at points $(1,1,1)$, $(1,0,0)$, and $(0,0,0)$, respectively. Show that they can be reduced to a couple, and find the magnitude and direction of the couple.

PROBLEM 10.3.12 A 60-lb weight is suspended from three strings, joined at point D, and attached to a circular ring. The diameter of the ring is 12 in., and the length of each string is 12 in. If $\alpha = \beta = 5\gamma/2$, determine the tension in each string.

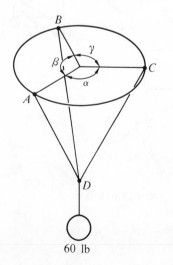

60 lb

What relationship must exist between dimensions (x_1, y_1, z_1) such that the force system given in the diagram may be reduced to a single force?

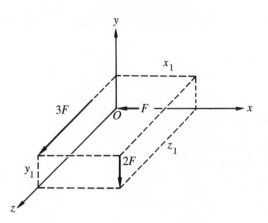

Replace the applied forces shown by a force acting at point A and a couple.

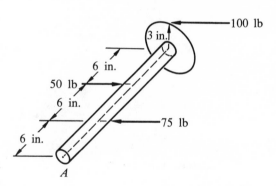

Replace the following force system by an equipollent system having one couple and a force at point $(1,1,1)$:   **PROBLEM 10.3.15**

$$\mathbf{F}_1 = 9\mathbf{i} - 2\mathbf{j} + 6\mathbf{k} \qquad \text{at } (5,0,-2)$$

$$\mathbf{F}_2 = 3\mathbf{j} - 2\mathbf{k} \qquad \text{at } (0,1,-2)$$

$$\mathbf{F}_3 = -6\mathbf{i} + 4\mathbf{j} - \mathbf{k} \qquad \text{at } (4,0,0)$$

$$\mathbf{C}_1 = 4\mathbf{i} - 2\mathbf{j} + 5\mathbf{k}$$

$$\mathbf{C}_2 = 3\mathbf{i} - \mathbf{j} + 2\mathbf{k}$$

Reduction of force systems

PROBLEM 10.3.16

Replace the forces shown by a force acting at point A and a couple.

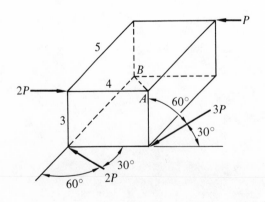

100 lb

50 lb

30°

6 ft

3 ft

6 ft   4 ft

3 ft

A

PROBLEM 10.3.17

Replace the forces shown by an equipollent system of two forces, one of which acts along AB, the diagonal of the block.

P

5

B

$2P$

4

A 60°

$3P$

3

30°

30°

60° $2P$

Section 10.4 Equilibrium of a rigid body

A light ladder rests on a rough floor and leans against a smooth wall. Rollers are installed at the base of the ladder, A and B, such that the ladder can roll along the x-direction without friction. A weight of 100 lb is hung on the ladder as shown. What is the minimum coefficient of friction between the roller and floor which prevents the base of the ladder from sliding in the y-direction?

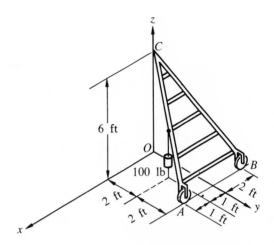

Solution

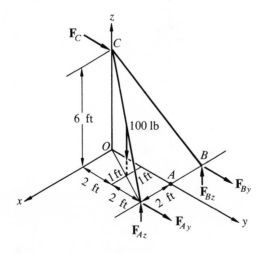

Equilibrium of a rigid body

$\Sigma \mathbf{F} = 0$:

$$0 = (F_C + F_{By} + F_{Ay})\mathbf{j} + (F_{Az} + F_{Bz} - 100)\mathbf{k}$$

$\Sigma \mathbf{M} = 0 = -\Sigma \mathbf{F}_i \times \mathbf{r}_i$:

$$0 = \begin{vmatrix} \mathbf{i} & \mathbf{j} & \mathbf{k} \\ 0 & 0 & -100 \\ 1 & -2 & 3 \end{vmatrix} + \begin{vmatrix} \mathbf{i} & \mathbf{j} & \mathbf{k} \\ 0 & F_C & 0 \\ 0 & -4 & 6 \end{vmatrix} + \begin{vmatrix} \mathbf{i} & \mathbf{j} & \mathbf{k} \\ 0 & F_{Ay} & F_{Az} \\ 2 & 0 & 0 \end{vmatrix}$$

$$+ \begin{vmatrix} \mathbf{i} & \mathbf{j} & \mathbf{k} \\ 0 & F_{By} & F_{Bz} \\ -2 & 0 & 0 \end{vmatrix}$$

that is,

$$(-200 + 6F_C)\mathbf{i} + (-100 + 2F_{Az} - 2F_{Bz})\mathbf{j}$$

$$+ (-2F_{Ay} + 2F_{By})\mathbf{k} = 0$$

Therefore,

$F_C + F_{By} + F_{Ay} = 0$	$2F_{Ay} = -F_C = \frac{200}{6}$
$F_{Az} + F_{Bz} = 100$	$F_{Ay} = F_{By} = \frac{50}{3}$ lb
$F_C = \frac{200}{6}$ lb	$2F_{Az} = 150$
$F_{Az} - F_{Bz} = 50$	$F_{Az} = 75$ lb
$F_{Ay} = F_{By}$	$F_{Bz} = 75 - 50 = 25$ lb

At A,

$$\min \mu = \frac{50}{3 \times 75} = \frac{2}{9}$$

at B,

$$\min \mu = \frac{50}{3 \times 25} = \frac{2}{3}$$

Therefore,

$$\min \mu = \frac{2}{3}$$

Determine the force (tension or compression) in member *AB* if the structure is in equilibrium under the given applied forces. The hinges at *A*, *B*, *C*, and *D* are smooth.

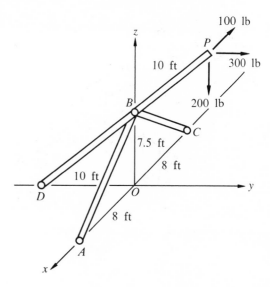

Determine the magnitude of force **P** in the *y*-direction which must be applied at *D* to lift weight *W* = 10 lb. Find the reactions at bearings *A* and *B* at the instant shown.

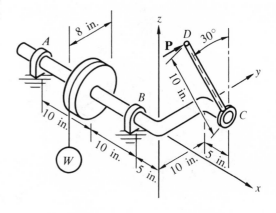

Equilibrium of a rigid body

Determine the reaction forces and moments at fixed end *A* for the system of forces shown.

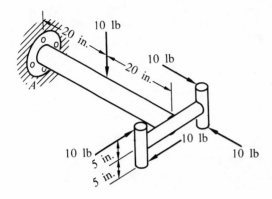

A 4- by 6-ft plate weighing 1,000 lb is lifted by three cables joined at point *D* directly above the center of the plate. Determine the tension in each cable.

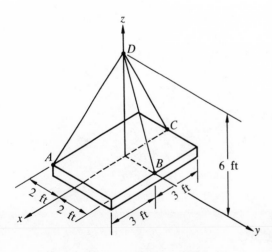

A door is made self-closing by attaching a 20-lb weight to it by means of cable *BC*. The door is held open by a force **F** applied normal to the door at *A*. Determine the magnitude of **F** as a function of *θ*.

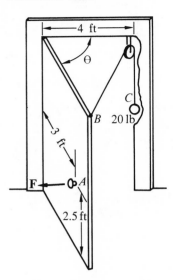

A man stands at point *A* of a "weightless" board resting on the ground. Determine the minimum force the man must exert to just raise himself off the ground.

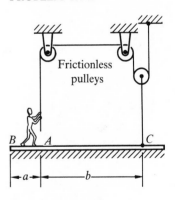

A beam weighing 100 lb is supported at its ends by two cables and is subjected to a lateral force of 1 lb at *C*. What are the horizontal displacements of points *A* and *B* when the beam is in equilibrium? Assume small displacements.

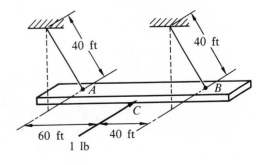

Equilibrium of a rigid body

PROBLEM 10.4.8

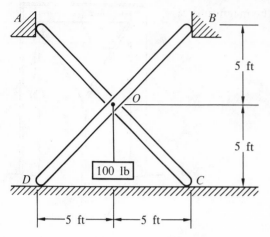

The surfaces at A, B, C, and D are frictionless. Determine the reactions at the contact points and the force exerted on member AOC at point O.

PROBLEM 10.4.9

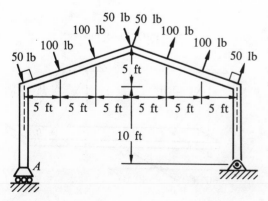

The roof of a building is subjected to in-plane loads as shown. Determine the resultant of the loading and its line of action. Find the reactions at A and B.

168

A ladder is placed on a frictionless floor. Neglecting the weight of the ladder, determine
(a) The reactions at D and E;
(b) The force in the tie rod BC;
(c) The force at hinge A.

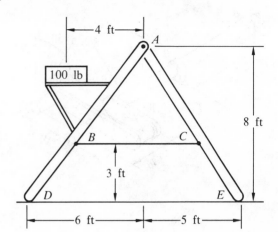

Neglecting the weight of the stand, find the reactions at A, B, and C. $W = 100$ lb, $\alpha = 20°$, $AB = BC = CA = 6$ ft.

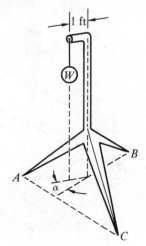

Equilibrium of a rigid body

A light crank in smooth bearings A and B is subjected to forces P_1 and P_2 as shown. Find the reaction forces at bearings A and B.

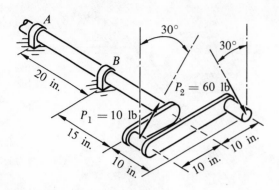

A uniform plate weighing 10 lb is welded to a weightless rod which can rotate in bearings A and B. Assuming that bearing A exerts no axial thrust, determine the tension in the cable and the components of the reactions at A and B. The cable is fixed at point C.

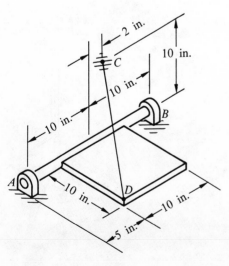

Find the tension in cables CA and CB, which support the vertical mast as shown. No moment is exerted on the mast by the support at O.

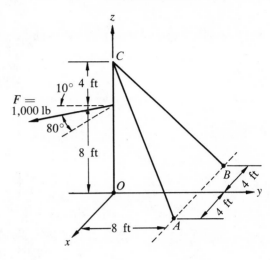

Two spheres of radius r and weight W are placed in a right circular cylindrical tube of inner radius R and weight W'. The cylinder is placed on a smooth surface with its axis vertical. If $R/2 < r < R$, what relation must exist between r and R to maintain the cylinder upright? Assume that all surfaces are frictionless.

A 100-lb load is suspended from corner B of a rigid section of pipe $ABCD$, which has been bent as shown. The pipe is supported by ball-and-socket joints A and D fastened to the wall and floor, respectively. A cable is attached between point E on the pipe and a point F on the wall. Determine the location of point F if the tension in the cable is to be minimum and the corresponding minimum value of the tension.

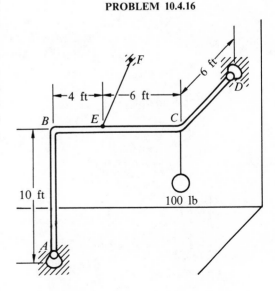

Equilibrium of a rigid body

Section 10.5 Displacements of a rigid body

At a given instant, points $O(0,0,0)$ ft and $P(1,1,1)$ ft in a rigid body have velocities $(\mathbf{i} + 2\mathbf{j} + 3\mathbf{k})$ ft/sec and $(4\mathbf{i} - \mathbf{j} + 3\mathbf{k})$ ft/sec, respectively. Is there a point of the rigid body at rest at this instant? Prove your answer.

Solution

$$\mathbf{v}_P = \mathbf{v}_O + \boldsymbol{\omega} \times \mathbf{r}$$

$$4\mathbf{i} - \mathbf{j} + 3\mathbf{k} = \mathbf{i} + 2\mathbf{j} + 3\mathbf{k} + \begin{vmatrix} \mathbf{i} & \mathbf{j} & \mathbf{k} \\ \omega_x & \omega_y & \omega_z \\ 1 & 1 & 1 \end{vmatrix}$$

$$0 = (-3 + \omega_y - \omega_z)\mathbf{i} + (+3 + \omega_z - \omega_x)\mathbf{j} + (\omega_x - \omega_y)\mathbf{k}$$

Thus,

$$\omega_x = \omega_y \qquad\qquad \omega_x = \omega_y = \omega$$

$$\omega_z - \omega_x = -3 \quad \text{or} \quad \omega_z = \omega - 3$$

$$\omega_y - \omega_z = 3$$

$$0 \overset{?}{=} \mathbf{v} = \mathbf{i} + 2\mathbf{j} + 3\mathbf{k} + \begin{vmatrix} \mathbf{i} & \mathbf{j} & \mathbf{k} \\ \omega & \omega & \omega - 3 \\ r_x & r_y & r_z \end{vmatrix}$$

There is no value of ω for which this equation permits a solution; therefore there is no point in the body at rest.

A wheel rolls in the $\mathbf{j}$-direction and slips in the $\mathbf{i}$-direction. Its center has a velocity $\mathbf{V} = 2\mathbf{i} + 10\mathbf{j}$ ft/sec. The diameter of the wheel is 1 ft. Find the pitch of the screw displacement.

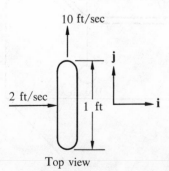

10 ft/sec

2 ft/sec

1 ft

Top view

172

A wheel rolls forward on a horizontal road without slipping. **PROBLEM 10.5.2**
The center of the wheel has a velocity of 2 ft/sec. Find the
velocity of the point on the rim at the one o'clock position.

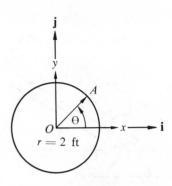

Prove that for any infinitesimal displacements of a point of a **PROBLEM 10.5.3**
rigid body, $\delta\mathbf{n} \cdot \delta\mathbf{s}$ is an invariant, where $\delta\mathbf{n}$ is an infinitesimal
rotation and $\delta\mathbf{s}$ is an infinitesimal displacement.

Small rotations of magnitudes $\delta\theta_1$, $\delta\theta_2$, and **PROBLEM 10.5.4**
$\delta\theta_3$ are applied to a cube about the diagonals
AQ, BQ, and CQ of three faces meeting at a
corner. Find the displacement of O. What is
the displacement of O if $\delta\theta_1 = \delta\theta_2 = \delta\theta_3$?

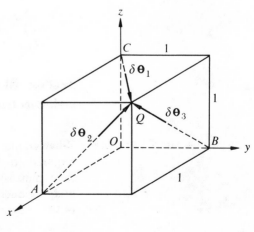

Displacements of a rigid body   *173*

PROBLEM 10.5.5

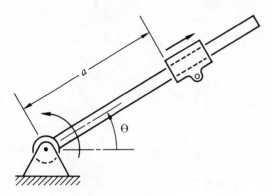

A slider moves along a rotating arm as shown. Find the axis of the screw displacement of the slider occurring in an infinitesimal time for the position shown.

PROBLEM 10.5.6

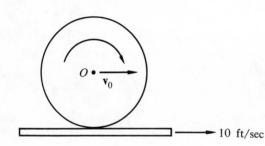

A wheel of radius 1 ft is rolling on a sliding board which is moving at 10 ft/sec and the center of the wheel has a velocity of 10 ft/sec relative to the board. Find the pitch and the axis of the screw motion of the wheel.

PROBLEM 10.5.7   Show that for a rigid body undergoing a general plane motion, there exists an axis of rotation for each instant.

Section 10.6   Generalized coordinates and constraints

SAMPLE PROBLEM   What is the minimum number of generalized coordinates required to describe the configuration of a rigid body in three-dimensional space? Is the configuration of the rigid body uniquely determined when the positions of two points of the body are specified? Explain your answer.

Solution

A rigid body in three-dimensional space has six degrees of freedom; therefore, six generalized coordinates are required to specify its configuration uniquely: for example, the position of one point of the body (x,y,z) and the three Eulerian angles (θ,ϕ,ψ) between body-fixed and space-fixed reference axes. To uniquely determine the configuration of the body, it is not enough to specify the position of two points (x_1,y_1,z_1) and (x_2,y_2,z_2) because the constraint equation

$$(x_1 - x_2)^2 + (y_1 - y_2)^2 + (z_1 - z_2)^2 = \text{const}$$

eliminates one of the six variables and thus leaves one coordinate required for the precise location undetermined.

The point P on a rigid body is constrained to move in the x-y plane. Choose a set of generalized coordinates to determine the configuration of the rigid body.

PROBLEM 10.6.1

Find two sets of generalized coordinates for each of the two-dimensional systems shown.

PROBLEM 10.6.2

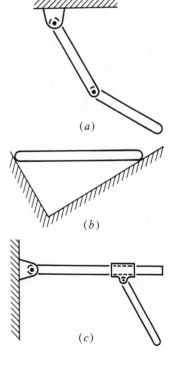

(a)

(b)

(c)

PROBLEM 10.6.3

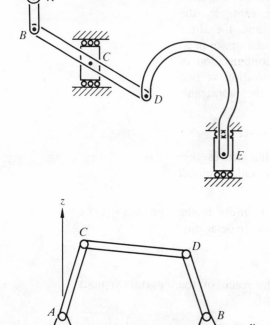

Determine the number of degrees of freedom for each of the systems shown. Choose a set of generalized coordinates for each case. In the first figure AB, BD, and DE are rigid bars. In the second figure AC, CD, and DB are rigid bars, A and B are ball-and-socket joints, and C and D are universal joints; motion occurs in three dimensions.

PROBLEM 10.6.4 Find a set of generalized coordinates for the system shown.

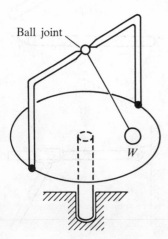

Statics in space

A bar of length l can move freely in the x-y plane. How many degrees of freedom does the bar have? If it is required that the two ends of the bar remain on curve $(x^2/a^2) + (y^2/b^2) = 1$, set up the equations of constraint. How many degrees of freedom does the bar now have?

PROBLEM 10.6.5

A straight rigid bar AB of length l is constrained to move in such a way that end A remains on surface $z = f(x,y)$, while end B remains on surface $z = g(x,y)$. How many degrees of freedom does the bar have? What are the equations of constraint?

PROBLEM 10.6.6

One end of a rigid rod is free to slide on the floor, while the other end is free to slide on a vertical wall. Determine the degrees of freedom of the rod and choose a set of generalized coordinates.

PROBLEM 10.6.7

A triangular plate has rotated from position OAB to $OA'B'$ as shown. Find the Eulerian angles of this rotation.

PROBLEM 10.6.8

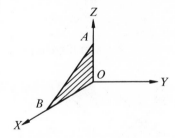

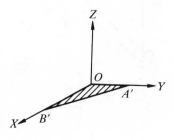

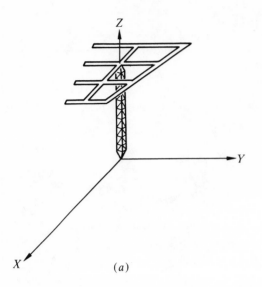

(a)

What are the Eulerian angles of the antenna at position *b* measured with reference to position *a*?

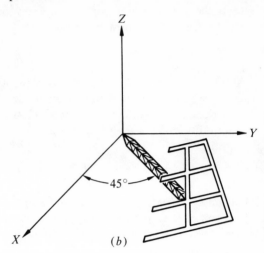

(b)

Section 10.7 Work and potential energy

SAMPLE PROBLEM

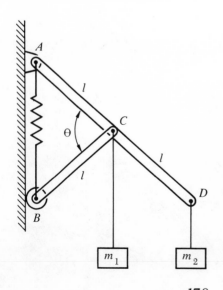

Spring *AB* has a spring constant *k* and an unstretched length $l/2$. Neglecting the weight of the links and friction forces, determine the value (s) of θ at the equilibrium position by the method of virtual work.

178

Solution

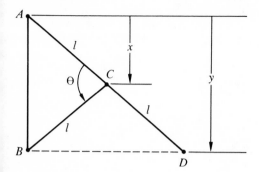

At the equilibrium position,

$$F_{\text{spring}} = \left(2l \sin \frac{\theta}{2} - \frac{l}{2} \right) k = F_s$$

$$x = l \sin \frac{\theta}{2} \qquad \delta x = \frac{l}{2} \cos \frac{\theta}{2} \, \delta\theta$$

$$y = 2l \sin \frac{\theta}{2} \qquad \delta y = l \cos \frac{\theta}{2} \, \delta\theta$$

$$\delta W = -F_s \, \delta y + m_1 g \, \delta x + m_2 g \, \delta y = 0$$

$$= -\left(2l \sin \frac{\theta}{2} - \frac{l}{2} \right) kl \cos \frac{\theta}{2} \, \delta\theta$$

$$+ m_1 g \frac{l}{2} \cos \frac{\theta}{2} \, \delta\theta + m_2 g \, l \cos \frac{\theta}{2} \, \delta\theta = 0$$

$$l \neq 0 \qquad \delta\theta \neq 0$$

Therefore, $\qquad \cos \dfrac{\theta}{2} = 0 \qquad \theta = \pi$

or $\qquad \sin \dfrac{\theta}{2} = \dfrac{1}{4} \left(1 + \dfrac{m_1 g + 2m_2 g}{lk} \right)$

Work and potential energy

PROBLEM 10.7.1 A ball weighing 10 lb is released from a height of 10 ft above the floor. The ball falls on top of a spring having a spring constant of 10 lb/in. and an unstretched length of 10 in. Neglecting air resistance, find the maximum deflection of the spring resulting from the impact.

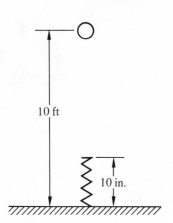

10 ft

10 in.

PROBLEM 10.7.2 A hammer weighing 200 lb is used to drive a pile into the soil. The hammer, which does not rebound, is always released from a fixed point initially located 30 ft above the top of the pile before it is struck. The pile descends a distance of 24 in. after five blows, moving the same distance during each blow. Neglecting the weight of the pile, find the average total resistive force exerted on the pile by the soil.

PROBLEM 10.7.3 The main drive shaft of a car weighing 2,000 lb turns at 120 rpm while the car is traveling at a speed of 25 mph up a road which makes an angle of $\sin^{-1} 0.003$ with the horizontal. Assume that all energy losses due to friction and air resistance can be neglected. Find the torque in the shaft and the elevation gain after 10 min of travel.

PROBLEM 10.7.4

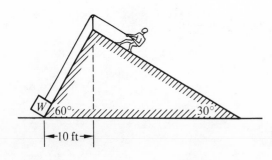

W 60° 30°

10 ft

A man pulls a weight of 100 lb along a frictionless surface by means of a weightless cable and a frictionless pulley, as shown. Assume that the man weighs 150 lb and he pulls at uniform speed. Find the tension in the cable by the concept of work and potential energy.

180

Two rollers weighing W_1 and W_2 lb ($W_1 > W_2$), respectively, are connected by a spring of negligible weight, spring constant k, and unstretched length d. If the rollers are placed on the inclined planes as shown, what is the distance l at equilibrium?

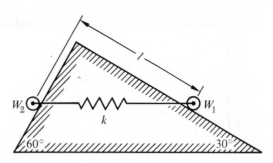

A follower attached to a spring of constant $k = 2$ lb/in. moves around a cam whose profile is $r = 10 - 3 \cos \theta$ in. The weight of the follower is 6 lb. The unstretched length l of the spring is 2 in. Find the equilibrium positions and determine if they are stable or unstable.

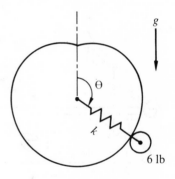

A 15-ft cable is fastened at A and B. Find the equilibrium position of pulley C and the corresponding tension in the cable. Assume that the cable and pulley are weightless and that the diameter of the pulley is negligibly small.

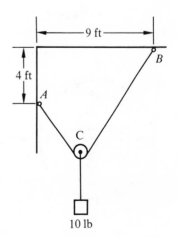

PROBLEM 10.7.8 A simple pendulum capable of full rotation is made of a weightless rigid bar and a mass m. Find the equilibrium positions and determine the stability at each position.

PROBLEM 10.7.9

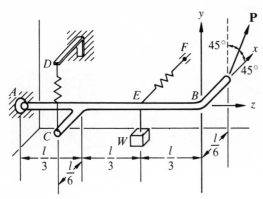

A weightless bar AB is attached to the wall at A by a ball joint such that the bar can rotate about A in all directions. Springs CD and EF are attached to the bar as shown. The system is in equilibrium under load W and force $\mathbf{P}$. Determine the magnitude of $\mathbf{P}$ and the forces in the springs by the method of virtual work.

PROBLEM 10.7.10

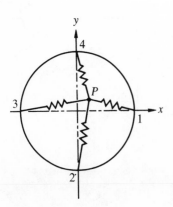

Four springs whose unstretched lengths are negligible and whose spring constants are 12 lb/in., 13 lb/in., 14 lb/in., and 15 lb/in., respectively, are attached to each other at point P. The other four ends are fixed to a rigid circular ring with a diameter of 40 in. Find the equilibrium position(s) in the plane of the ring and the force in each spring by the potential energy method.

Find the magnitude of the force **P** which maintains in equilibrium the two-dimensional system shown. Use the method of virtual work.

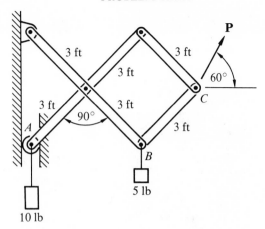

The equilibrium position of the system shown occurs when the spring is horizontal. Determine the force in the spring by the method of virtual work and determine the potential energy stored in the spring. The uniform bar weighs W lb.

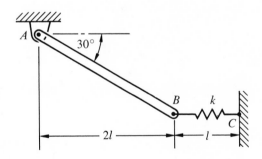

A particle moves on a frictionless surface whose equation is $z = A[(x-a)^2 + (b-y)^3]$, where A and a,b are positive constants. Find the equilibrium position(s) and the stability of the position(s).

Work and potential energy   *183*

PROBLEM 10.7.14

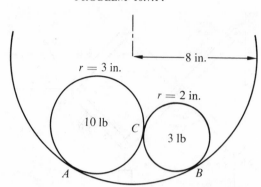

r = 3 in.

r = 2 in.

10 lb

C

3 lb

A

B

8 in.

Two balls are placed in a frictionless bowl as shown. Find the equilibrium position and the reaction forces at contact points A, B, and C.

PROBLEM 10.7.15

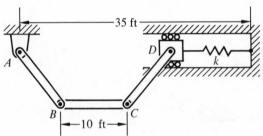

35 ft

D

k

A

B

C

10 ft

Three links, 10 ft long and weighing 200 lb each, are hinged together such that they can move only in a vertical plane. End A is hinged to the ceiling; end D slides in a frictionless slot and is attached to a spring having a constant of 10 lb/ft and an unstretched length of 5 ft. Using the potential energy method determine the force in the spring.

PROBLEM 10.7.16

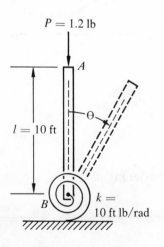

P = 1.2 lb

A

θ

l = 10 ft

B

k = 10 ft lb/rad

A weightless bar AB of length 10 ft is attached to the floor at B by a torsion spring with a spring constant of 10 ft-lb/radians. The bar is restrained so as to move in a single plane. Find the equilibrium positions under a vertical load of 1.2 lb at point A. Discuss the stability at each position. Discuss the problem for $P < 1$ lb.

A plank of uniform thickness t is balanced on top of a cylinder of radius R. The cylinder is fixed and the plank rolls on the cylinder without sliding. What relation must exist between t and R to ensure stability of the equilibrium position(s)?

A cross-sectional view of a uniform door equipped with two springs is shown in the figure. The weight of the door is W; all other members are assumed to be of negligible weight. The upper end of the door moves in a frictionless horizontal groove. The unstretched length of the spring is $l - e$. Find the spring constant k which will make the closed position a position of neutral equilibrium.

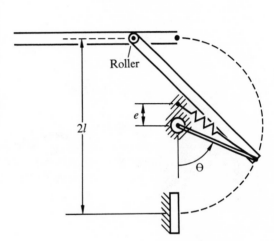

A particle P that can move in a plane is attracted by masses M_1 and M_2, fixed at A and B, respectively. Assume that the attractive forces follow the universal law of gravitation. Determine the position(s) of equilibrium and the stability of the equilibrium position(s).

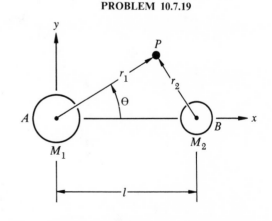

Discuss the stability of the equilibrium positions obtained in the sample problem at the beginning of this section.

Work and potential energy

185

KINEMATICS: KINETIC ENERGY AND ANGULAR MOMENTUM

Section 11.1 Kinematics of a particle

SAMPLE PROBLEM A particle moves with constant speed v along a path given parametrically by $x = e^r$, $y = \sin r$, and $z = r^2$. Find the velocity and the acceleration of the particle as a function of time.

Solution

$$\mathbf{R} = x\mathbf{i} + y\mathbf{j} + z\mathbf{k} = e^r\mathbf{i} + \sin r\mathbf{j} + r^2\mathbf{k}$$

$$\mathbf{v} = \frac{d\mathbf{R}}{dt} = (e^r\mathbf{i} + \cos r\mathbf{j} + 2r\mathbf{k})\frac{dr}{dt}$$

$$\frac{ds}{dt} = v = \frac{\sqrt{dx^2 + dy^2 + dz^2}}{dt} = \frac{dr}{dt}\sqrt{e^{2r} + \cos^2 r + 4r^2}$$

Therefore,

$$\mathbf{v} = (e^r\mathbf{i} + \cos r\mathbf{j} + 2r\mathbf{k})\frac{v}{\sqrt{e^{2r} + \cos^2 r + 4r^2}}$$

$$\mathbf{a} = \frac{d\mathbf{v}}{dt} = \frac{v(e^r\mathbf{i} - \sin r\mathbf{j} + 2\mathbf{k})}{\sqrt{e^{2r} + \cos^2 r + 4r^2}}\frac{dr}{dt}$$

$$-\frac{1}{2}\frac{v(e^r\mathbf{i} + \cos r\mathbf{i} + 2r\mathbf{k})}{(e^{2r} + \cos^2 r + 4r^2)^{3/2}}(2e^{2r} - 2\cos r \sin r + 8r)\frac{dr}{dt}$$

$$= \frac{v^2(e^r\mathbf{i} - \sin r\mathbf{j} + 2\mathbf{k})}{e^{2r} + \cos^2 r + 4r^2}$$

$$-\frac{v^2}{2} \frac{(2e^{2r} - \sin 2r + 8r)}{(e^{2r} + \cos^2 r + 4r^2)^2} (e^r\mathbf{i} + \cos r\mathbf{j} + 2r\mathbf{k})$$

A particle moves from rest from point $(2,1,0)$ with acceleration   **PROBLEM 11.1.1**
components $a_x = 2 + t$, $a_y = t^2$, and $a_z = t^3 - 2$. Find the
position vector as a function of t.

Find the acceleration of a particle moving along a diameter   **PROBLEM 11.1.2**
of a disk at constant speed v relative to the disk while the
disk is turning at constant angular velocity ω about the
central axis normal to the disk.

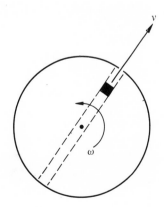

PROBLEM 11.1.3 A particle moves at a constant speed of 5 ft/sec along a path given by $y = 10e^{-2x}$, where x and y are in ft. Find the acceleration of the particle when $x = 2$ ft.

PROBLEM 11.1.4 The vector from the origin to a moving particle is $\mathbf{R} = t^2\mathbf{i} + t^3\mathbf{j} - t^4\mathbf{k}$. Find the velocity of the particle when $t = 2$. What is the component of the velocity in the direction of the vector $6\mathbf{i} - 2\mathbf{j} + 3\mathbf{k}$? What is the acceleration of the particle at $t = 2$? What are the tangential and normal components of this acceleration?

PROBLEM 11.1.5 A particle travels along a space curve at constant speed v. The curve is given by $x = ar$, $y = br^2$, $z = cr^3$, where a, b, and c are constants. Find the velocity and acceleration of the particle at point (a,b,c).

PROBLEM 11.1.6 A particle moves along a helix at constant speed v. The equation of the helix in cylindrical coordinates is given by $r = \text{const} = a$; $z = p\ 0/2\pi$, $p = \text{const}$. Calculate the cylindrical components of the velocity and acceleration.

PROBLEM 11.1.7 A particle moves along a helix defined by the equation $r = a = \text{const}$; $z = p\,\theta/2\pi$, $p = \text{const}$. If the particle moves along the curve with acceleration of constant magnitude, find the position of the particle as a function of time.

PROBLEM 11.1.8 A particle can move freely on the surface of a sphere. Express the velocity and acceleration of the particle in terms of
(a) Spherical coordinates;
(b) Cylindrical coordinates;
(c) Cartesian coordinates.

PROBLEM 11.1.9 Derive an expression for the radius of curvature of a plane curve in polar coordinates (see Sec. 4.1 of Synge and Griffith).

A particle travels at constant speed v along the plane curve $r = A\theta$, A = const. Find the normal and tangential components of acceleration. Find the acceleration in cylindrical coordinates (see Prob. 11.1.9).

PROBLEM 11.1.10

A particle travels along a parabola such that the horizontal component of the velocity, $\dot{x}$, remains constant. Find the acceleration of the particle as a function of position.

PROBLEM 11.1.11

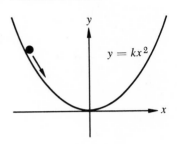

A particle moves with constant speed v along a space curve given by

PROBLEM 11.1.12

$$x = \cos\theta \qquad y = \sin\theta \qquad z = \theta$$

Find the velocity and acceleration of the particle as functions of θ.

Section 11.2 Kinematics of a rigid body

Gear B is fixed in space and gear A turns about line OA with angular velocity ω. Find the angular velocity of gear C which is attached at O by a ball joint.

SAMPLE PROBLEM

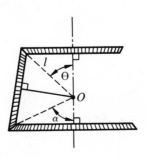

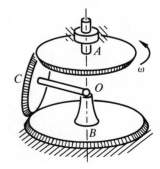

Solution

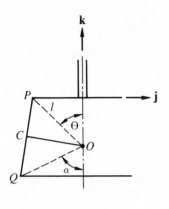

$$\mathbf{v}_P = \boldsymbol{\omega} \times (-l \sin \theta)\mathbf{j} = \omega l \sin \theta\mathbf{i}$$
$$= \boldsymbol{\omega}_C \times (-l \sin \theta\mathbf{j} + l \cos \theta\mathbf{k})$$

$$\begin{vmatrix} \mathbf{i} & \mathbf{j} & \mathbf{k} \\ \omega_{Cx} & \omega_{Cy} & \omega_{Cz} \\ 0 & -l \sin \theta & l \cos \theta \end{vmatrix} = \omega l \sin \theta\mathbf{i}$$

or
$$\left. \begin{aligned} \omega_{Cy}\, l \cos \theta + \omega_{Cz}\, l \sin \theta &= \omega l \sin \theta \\ \omega_{Cx} &= 0 \end{aligned} \right\} \tag{1}$$

$$\mathbf{v}_Q = 0 = \begin{vmatrix} \mathbf{i} & \mathbf{j} & \mathbf{k} \\ 0 & \omega_{Cy} & \omega_{Cz} \\ 0 & -l \sin \alpha & -l \cos \alpha \end{vmatrix}$$

$$= (-\omega_{Cy}\, l \cos \alpha + \omega_{Cz}\, l \sin \alpha)\mathbf{i} \tag{2}$$

Thus
$$\omega_{Cy} = \omega_{Cz} \tan \alpha$$
$$\omega_{Cz}(\cos \theta \tan \alpha + \sin \theta) = \omega \sin \theta$$

Therefore,
$$\omega_{Cz} = \frac{\omega \sin \theta}{\cos \theta \tan \alpha + \sin \theta} \qquad \omega_{Cy} = \frac{\omega \sin \theta \tan \alpha}{\cos \theta \tan \alpha + \sin \theta}$$

PROBLEM 11.2.1 A roller moves down an inclined plane at constant speed $v = 10$ ft/sec. The rod OAP moves with the roller but is constrained to remain vertical and rotates about OA at angular speed $\omega = 4$ radians/sec. What is the velocity of point P at the instant AP is in the plane of $\mathbf{v}$ and OA?

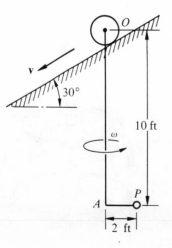

190

The helicopter blade shown rotates about the vertical axis at constant angular speed ω. The blade oscillates about a neutral position θ_0 such that θ is given by $\theta = \theta_0 + \theta_A \sin mt$, where θ_A is the amplitude of the oscillation. Find the velocity and acceleration of the tip of the blade for any value of θ.

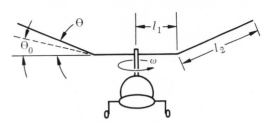

Let (x, y, z) be a set of axes fixed in a rigid body which moves with angular velocity ω, having components $(\omega_x, \omega_y, \omega_z)$ relative to this set of axes. If $\omega_x = \omega_z = 0$, find the components of ω along fixed axes (X, Y, Z) in terms $(\omega_x, \omega_y, \omega_z)$ and the Eulerian angles θ, ϕ, and ψ.

A right circular cone of height h and base radius a rolls on a horizontal surface without slipping such that the line of contact rotates about the z-axis at constant angular speed ω. Find the angular velocity Ω of the cone and the velocity v_A of the highest point on the base.

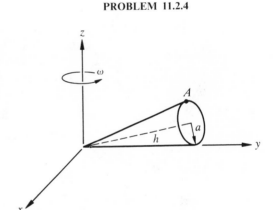

Two points A and B of a rigid body are located 4 in. apart. At the instant under consideration,

$$v_A = (3\mathbf{i} - 2\mathbf{j} + 4\mathbf{k}) \text{ in./sec}$$

$$v_B = (3\mathbf{i} + 6\mathbf{j} - 2\mathbf{k}) \text{ in./sec}$$

$$a_A = (2\mathbf{i} + 5\mathbf{k}) \text{ in./sec}^2$$

$$\frac{d\omega}{dt} = \mathbf{i} + 3\mathbf{j} \text{ radians/sec}^2$$

$$\omega_x = 0$$

Find the acceleration of point B.

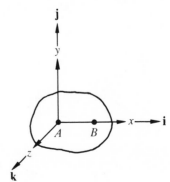

Kinetics of a rigid body

191

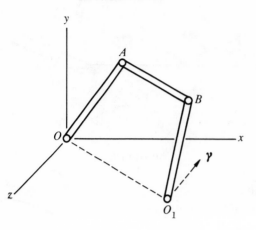

In the space linkage shown, OA turns about the z-axis and O_1B turns about the line in the xz-plane characterized by unit vector γ. Let $\mathbf{\Omega}_2$, $\mathbf{\Omega}_3$, and $\mathbf{\Omega}_4$ be the angular velocities of $\overline{OA}$, $\overline{AB}$, and $\overline{O_1B}$, respectively. Let $\vec{OO_1} = \mathbf{R}_1$, $\vec{OA} = \mathbf{R}_2$, $\vec{AB} = \mathbf{R}_3$, and $\vec{O_1B} = \mathbf{R}_4$. Show that:

$$\mathbf{\Omega}_3 = \frac{1}{R_3{}^2}\left[\mathbf{\Omega}_2(\mathbf{k} \times \mathbf{R}_2) \times \mathbf{R}_3\right.$$

$$\left. - \mathbf{\Omega}_4(\gamma \times \mathbf{R}_4) \times \mathbf{R}_3\right]$$

PROBLEM 11.2.7

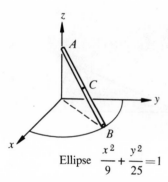

Ellipse $\dfrac{x^2}{9} + \dfrac{y^2}{25} = 1$

A rigid rod is constrained such that one end moves along the z-axis while the other end moves along the curve $(x^2/9) + (y^2/25) = 1$. What is the velocity of the center of the rod when the end on the z-axis is at $z = 3$ in., has a velocity of $\dot{z} = 2$ in./sec, and $x > 0$, $y > 0$? The length of the rod is 5 in.

PROBLEM 11.2.8

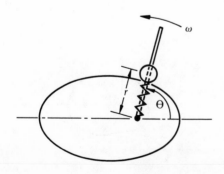

A roller follows a cam such that its center traces an ellipse given by $r = P/(1 + a\cos\theta)$. The roller slides along a rod which turns with constant angular velocity ω about point $r = 0$. Find the velocity and acceleration of the center of the roller as a function of θ.

Kinetic energy and angular momentum

A rod OP is pivoted at point O and rests on a cylindrical roller as shown. The roller moves to the left with a constant velocity of 5 ft/sec. What are the angular velocity and angular acceleration of the rod when $\theta = 30°$?

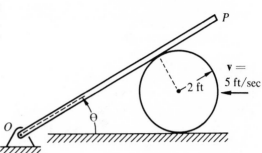

The differential of a car is designed such that the rear wheels can rotate about their axes BB and CC at different angular speeds ω_1 and ω_2, respectively. The two bevel gears attached to the wheel axis have radius R, and the two mating gears have radius r and rotate about their axes at angular speeds ω_A and $-\omega_A$, respectively. If the drive shaft rotates about the wheel axes at angular speed Ω, show that $2\Omega = \omega_1 + \omega_2$ and $2\omega_A = \frac{R}{r}(\omega_2 - \omega_1)$.

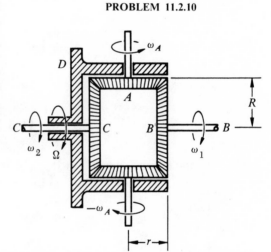

Cone A and cone B both turn about the x-axis with angular speed ω, but in opposite directions. Cone C rolls between A and B without slipping. Find the angular velocity of cone C.

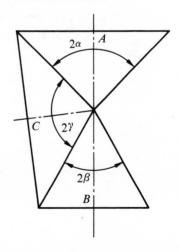

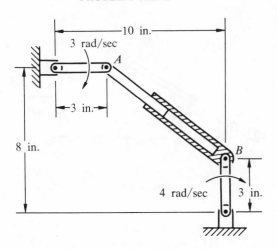

Find the instantaneous angular velocity of the telescoping link *AB* at the instant indicated in the figure.

Section 11.3   Moments and products of inertia

SAMPLE PROBLEM   Find the moments of inertia and products of inertia of the thin uniform triangular plate of mass *M* about the axes shown.

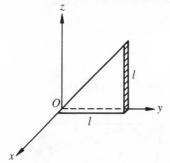

Solution

The mass per unit area is

$$\rho = \frac{M}{\frac{1}{2} l^2} = \frac{2M}{l^2}$$

$$y = l - z$$

194

Kinetic energy and angular momentum

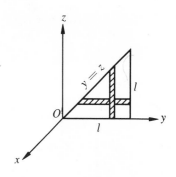

$$I_{yy} = \int_0^l \rho y z^2 \, dz = \frac{2M}{l^2} \int_0^l z^2(l - z) \, dz$$

$$= \frac{2M}{l^2} \left[\frac{lz^3}{3} - \frac{z^4}{4} \right]_0^l = \frac{M}{6} l^2$$

$$I_{xx} = \frac{1}{2} \iint_0 (y^2 + z^2)\rho \, dy \, dz = \frac{1}{2} \int_0^l \left(y^2 z + \frac{z^3}{3} \right) \Big|_0^l \frac{2M}{l^2} \, dy$$

$$= \frac{1}{2} \int_0^l \left(y^2 l + \frac{l^3}{3} \right) \frac{2M}{l^2} \, dy = \frac{M}{l^2} \left(\frac{y^3 l}{3} + \frac{l^3 y}{3} \right) \Big|_0^l$$

$$= \frac{2}{3} M l^2$$

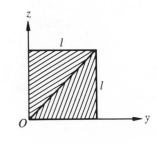

$$I_{zz} = \int_0^l \rho z y^2 \, dy = \int_0^l \frac{2M}{l^2} y^3 \, dy = \frac{2M}{l^3} \frac{y^4}{4} \Big|_0^l = \frac{1}{2} M l^2$$

$$I_{yz} = \int_0^l \int_0^y z y' \rho \, dz \, dy' = \int_0^l \left(\frac{z^2 y'}{2} \right) \Big|_0^y \frac{2M}{l^2} \, dy$$

$$= \int_0^l \frac{M}{l^2} \frac{y^3}{2} \, dy = \frac{M}{8} l^2$$

$$I_{xy} = I_{xz} = 0$$

A communications satellite is made of two spherical bodies as shown. The radius of the larger body is 20 ft, its mass is 60 slugs, and its moment of inertia about any diameter is 5,000 slug-ft^2. The radius of the smaller body is 10 ft, its mass is 20 slugs, and its moment of inertia about any diameter is 2,000 slug-ft^2. Find the inertia tensor for a set of axes at the center of mass of the satellite, where one axis connects the mass centers of the two spheres.

PROBLEM 11.3.1

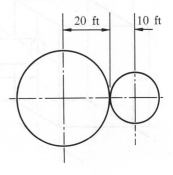

PROBLEM 11.3.2   Find the moment of inertia of the homogeneous solid cylinder about the x-axis and y-axis.

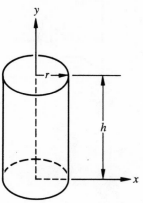

PROBLEM 11.3.3

Find the moments and products of inertia with respect to axes x, y, and z. The body is homogeneous and its weight density is 500 lb/ft^3.

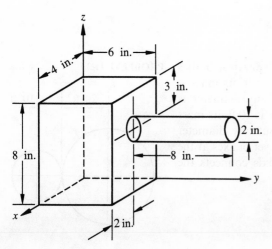

Kinetic energy and angular momentum

Find the moment of inertia of the solid cylinder about the x-axis and the y-axis. The mass density of the cylinder varies linearly from ρ_1 at $y = 0$ to ρ_2 at $y = h$.

PROBLEM 11.3.4

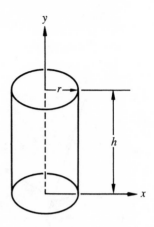

Find the area moment of inertia of the sector A about the x-axis.

PROBLEM 11.3.5

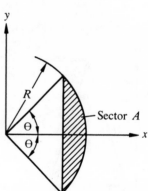

The momental ellipsoid at the center of mass of a homogeneous right circular cylinder is a sphere. The radius of the cylinder is a. What is the length of the cylinder?

PROBLEM 11.3.6

Find the equation of the momental ellipsoid of the homogeneous thin rectangular plate about the corner O. The thickness of the plate is t and the mass density is ρ.

PROBLEM 11.3.7

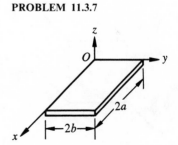

PROBLEM 11.3.8 Find the values of the principal moments of inertia of the thin rectangular plate of Prob. 11.3.7 about the corner O.

PROBLEM 11.3.9 The total mass of the homogeneous right circular cone is M. Find the moment of inertia of the cone about the x-axis and the z-axis.

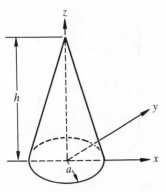

PROBLEM 11.3.10 The total mass of the homogeneous right circular cone is M. Find the moments of inertia about slant height l and about axis AA, which passes through the vertex and is perpendicular to the axis of the cone.

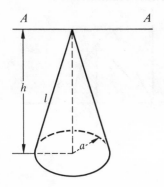

PROBLEM 11.3.11 Find the directions of the principal axes, and the values of the corresponding principal moments of inertia, of a homogeneous solid cube about one of its corners. The cube has a total mass M and a side length a.

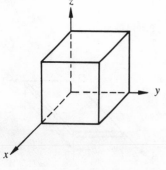

Kinetic energy and angular momentum

Find the moment of inertia of a solid homogeneous cube about the line characterized by the unit vector $\lambda(l, m, n)$ passing through one of its corners. The cube has a total mass M and a side length a.

PROBLEM 11.3.12

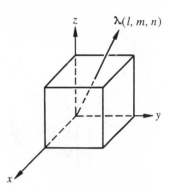

What is the moment of inertia about diagonal AB of a homogeneous rectangular parallelepiped of mass m?

PROBLEM 11.3.13

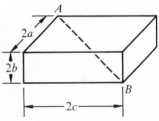

Find the moment of inertia of the uniform thin plate about the x-axis and the y-axis. The mass density is 0.1 slug/in.³ and the thickness is 0.1 in. The plate has five circular holes as shown.

PROBLEM 11.3.14

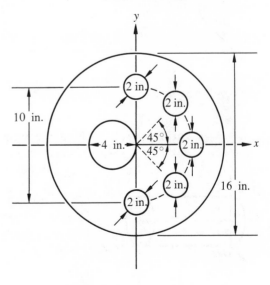

Moments and products of inertia   *199*

PROBLEM 11.3.15

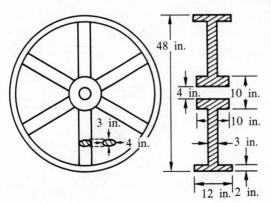

Determine the moment of inertia with respect to the axis of rotation of the cast-iron flywheel shown. The weight density of cast iron is 500 lb/ft³.

PROBLEM 11.3.16

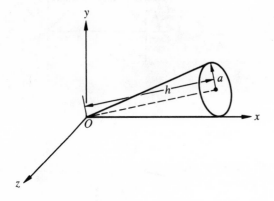

Find the product of inertia I_{xy} of the uniform right circular cone of base radius a, height h, and mass M.

PROBLEM 11.3.17 Find the principal moments of inertia of a uniform right circular cylinder at the point O shown. Mass = 6 slugs, $a = \frac{1}{2}$ ft, and $h = 1$ ft.

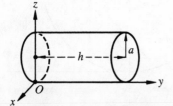

Kinetic energy and angular momentum

Find the principal moments of inertia of the uniform triangular block of mass M at the corner O.

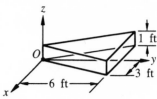

Section 11.4 Kinetic energy

Determine the kinetic energy of the uniform
circular disk of mass M at the instant shown.

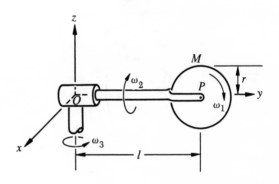

Solution

The angular velocity of the disk is

$$\boldsymbol{\omega} = \omega_3 \mathbf{k} - \omega_2 \mathbf{j} - \omega_1 \mathbf{i}$$

The velocity of the mass center of the disk is

$$\mathbf{v}_P = (\omega_1 \mathbf{k}) \times (l\mathbf{j}) = -\omega_1 l\mathbf{i}$$

$$A = I_{xx} = \tfrac{1}{2} Mr^2 \qquad B = I_{yy} = \tfrac{1}{4} Mr^2 = C = I_{zz}$$

$$T = \tfrac{1}{2} (M \, \mathbf{v}_P \cdot \mathbf{v}_P + A \, \omega_1{}^2 + B \, \omega_2{}^2 + C \, \omega_3{}^2)$$

$$= \frac{M}{2} \left(\omega_1{}^2 l^2 + \frac{r^2}{2} \omega_1{}^2 + \frac{r^2}{4} \omega_2{}^2 + \frac{r^2}{4} \omega_3{}^2 \right)$$

Kinetic energy   *201*

PROBLEM 11.4.1 Express the kinetic energy of a particle in terms of Cartesian, cylindrical, and spherical coordinates.

PROBLEM 11.4.2 Find the kinetic energy of a homogeneous solid disk of mass m and radius r that rolls without slipping along a straight line. The center of the disk moves with constant velocity $\mathbf{v}$.

PROBLEM 11.4.3 A homogeneous solid sphere of mass M and radius R is fixed at a point O on its surface by a ball joint. Find the kinetic energy of the sphere for the case of general motion.

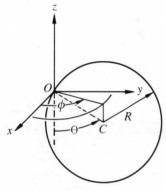

PROBLEM 11.4.4

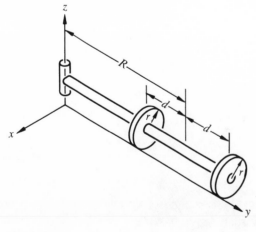

Two uniform circular disks, each of mass M and radius r, are mounted on the same shaft as shown. The shaft turns about the z-axis, while the two disks roll on the xy-plane without slipping. Prove that the ratio of the kinetic energies of the two disks is

$$\frac{6(R + d)^2 + r^2}{6(R - d)^2 + r^2}$$

Kinetic energy and angular momentum

A disk with arm OA is attached to a socket joint at O. The moment of inertia of the disk and arm about axis OA is I and the total mass is M, with the center of gravity at G. The disk rolls inside a cylinder whose radius is 4.8 in. Find the kinetic energy of the disk when the line of contact turns around the cylinder at 10 cps.

PROBLEM 11.4.5

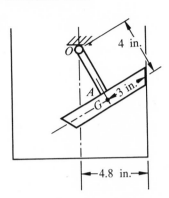

A uniform circular disk of radius a and mass M is mounted on a weightless shaft CD of length b. The shaft is normal to the disk at its center C. The disk rolls on the xy-plane without slipping, with point D remaining at the origin. Determine the kinetic energy of the disk if shaft CD rotates about the z-axis with constant angular speed n.

PROBLEM 11.4.6

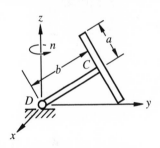

A homogeneous solid right circular cone rolls on a plane without slipping. The line of contact turns at constant angular speed Ω about the z-axis. Find the kinetic energy of the cone.

PROBLEM 11.4.7

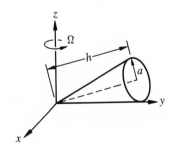

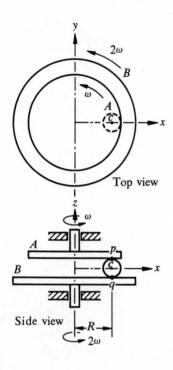

PROBLEM 11.4.8 A solid homogeneous sphere of radius r and mass M rolls between two parallel rotating disks as shown. Disk A has an angular velocity ω about the z-axis and disk B has an angular velocity 2ω about the z-axis. At a certain instant there is no slipping at contact points p and q and the ball has no angular velocity about line pq. Find the kinetic energy of the ball at that instant.

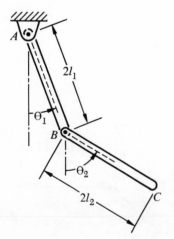

PROBLEM 11.4.9 Uniform bars AB and BC, each of mass M, are hinged at A and B such that they can move only in a plane. Using θ_1 and θ_2 as generalized coordinates, find the kinetic energy of the system.

Kinetic energy and angular momentum

A particle of mass m slides along one radius of a circular platform of mass M. At the instant shown, the platform has an angular velocity ω and the particle has a velocity $\mathbf{v}$ relative to the platform. Determine the kinetic energy and the angular momentum of the system about point O.

PROBLEM 11.4.10

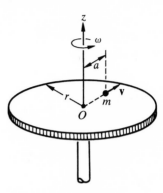

A pendulum consists of a uniform rod of mass m and a bob of mass $2m$. The pendulum is released from rest at position A as shown. What is the kinetic energy of the system at the lowest position? What is the velocity of the bob at the lowest position?

PROBLEM 11.4.11

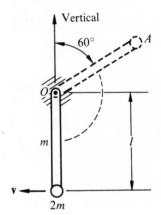

Section 11.5 Angular momentum

Find the angular momentum (moment of linear momentum relative to a fixed frame of reference) of the disk in the sample problem at the beginning of Sec. 11.4 about its mass center P and also about the base point O.

SAMPLE PROBLEM

Solution

The angular momentum about P is

$$\mathbf{h}_P = I_{xx}\omega_x\mathbf{i} + I_{yy}\omega_y\mathbf{j} + I_{zz}\omega_z\mathbf{k}$$

$$= Mr^2 \left(\frac{\omega_1}{2}\mathbf{i} + \frac{\omega_2}{4}\mathbf{j} + \frac{\omega_3}{4}\mathbf{k} \right)$$

The angular momentum about O is

$$\mathbf{h}_O = \mathbf{h}_P + \mathbf{r}_P \times M\,\mathbf{v}_P$$

$$= Mr^2\left(\frac{\omega_1}{2}\mathbf{i} + \frac{\omega_2}{4}\mathbf{j} + \frac{\omega_3}{4}\mathbf{k}\right) + Ml\mathbf{j} \times (-\omega_1 l\mathbf{i})$$

$$= Mr^2\left[\frac{\omega_1}{2}\mathbf{i} + \frac{\omega_2}{4}\mathbf{j} + \left(\frac{\omega_3}{4} + \frac{l^2\omega_1}{r^2}\right)\mathbf{k}\right]$$

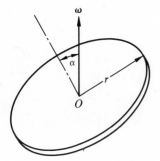

PROBLEM 11.5.1 A disk of mass M and radius r turns at angular speed ω about a fixed axis through its center O. The axis makes an angle α with the line normal to the disk. Find the angular momentum of the disk about O.

PROBLEM 11.5.2 For a rigid body with one fixed point, prove that the smaller angle between the angular velocity vector and the angular momentum vector about the fixed point is always acute.

PROBLEM 11.5.3 Find the angular momentum ⸴of the disk in Prob. 11.4.6 about the origin.

Kinetic energy and angular momentum

A uniform rod of length $2a$ and mass M is attached to a ball-and-socket joint at point O. It moves at constant angular speed describing a cone of constant half-angle α. The rod completes one revolution in time T. Find the magnitude and direction of the angular momentum.

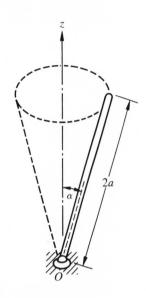

A uniform solid cube of mass M rotates about the x-axis with angular velocity ω. Find the angular momentum $\mathbf{h}$ about point O. Does $\mathbf{h}$ lie in the direction of ω?

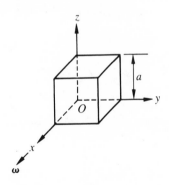

A uniform disk turns about an axis fixed in a rotating gimbal as shown. At which position relative to the gimbal will the angular momentum of the disk about O be parallel with its angular velocity? Prove your answer.

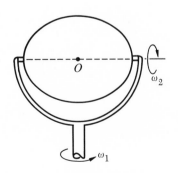

METHODS
OF DYNAMICS
IN SPACE

Section 12.1 Motion of a particle

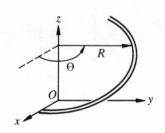

A particle of mass m is attracted toward the origin by a force with magnitude $(mK)/r^2$ where K is a constant and r is the distance between the particle and the center of attraction. The particle is constrained to move in a frictionless tube which lies along the space curve given by

$$\left. \begin{array}{l} z = 5\theta \\[2ex] R = 1 + \tfrac{1}{2}\theta \end{array} \right\} \quad \text{in cylindrical coordinates}$$

If the particle was at rest when $z = 10$, what is the velocity of the particle at $z = 0$?

Solution

The force is derivable from a potential, therefore

$$F = -\frac{mK}{r^2}$$

$$V = \int_r^\infty F\, dr = -\frac{mK}{r}$$

208

CHAPTER 12

Since no energy has been supplied from other sources,

$$T_0 + V_0 = T + V$$

At $z = 10, \theta = 2, R = 2$:

$$T_0 = 0 - V_0 = \frac{mK}{r} = \frac{mK}{\sqrt{z^2 + R^2}} = \frac{mK}{\sqrt{10^2 + 2^2}} = \frac{mK}{\sqrt{104}}$$

At $z = \theta = 0, R = 1$:

$$T = \frac{1}{2} mv^2 \qquad -V = \frac{mK}{\sqrt{0^2 + 1}} = mK$$

Therefore

$$\frac{1}{2} mv^2 = mK - \frac{mK}{\sqrt{104}} \qquad v = \sqrt{2K\left(1 - \frac{1}{\sqrt{104}}\right)}$$

PROBLEM 12.1.1

A particle under gravity is released from rest in a fluid which resists motion with a force given by $-k\dot{x}^n$, where k and n are positive constants. What is the terminal velocity of the particle?

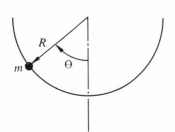

PROBLEM 12.1.2 A particle of mass m slides without friction along an arc of a circle of radius R located in a vertical plane. The particle starts from rest at a position such that the radius makes an angle θ_0 with the vertical. Find the reaction between the particle and the curve as a function of the angle θ.

PROBLEM 12.1.3 A particle of mass m is attracted to a fixed line by a force directed along the perpendicular from the particle to the line. The magnitude of the force is proportional to this perpendicular distance. Prove that the particle moves on an elliptical cylinder.

PROBLEM 12.1.4 A satellite was launched such that burnout occurred at an altitude of 1,780 miles with a burnout velocity parallel to the earth's surface and equal to 13,700 mph. Assuming that the earth is a perfect sphere with a radius of 4,000 miles, find the maximum and minimum height of the satellite orbit relative to the earth's surface. (Assume $g = 32$ ft/sec^2 at the earth's surface.)

PROBLEM 12.1.5 A ball of mass $M = 0.01$ slug and volume $V = 0.4$ in.^{3} is released from rest in a fluid whose weight density is 0.05 lb/in.^{3} The ball sinks under gravitational force. If the total frictional force exerted on the particle is equal to $0.1v$ lb, where v in ft/sec is the speed of the particle, determine the expression for the time history of the motion of the particle, including the effect of buoyancy.

PROBLEM 12.1.6 A particle slides in a frictionless tube OB, which rotates with constant velocity ω about a horizontal axis through O. If the particle is initially at rest relative to the tube and $r = a$, $\theta = 0$ when $t = 0$, find the reaction between the particle and the tube as a function of time.

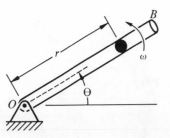

Methods of dynamics in space

A bullet of mass m is fired horizontally with muzzle velocity $\mathbf{v}$. Resistance to motion along the line of sight to the target, the x-axis, is $F = c\dot{x}^2$. A cross wind perpendicular to the line of sight causes a horizontal deflection d from the line of sight to the target when the range is R. Find an expression for the constant force exerted on the bullet by the cross wind. Neglect the effect of gravity.

PROBLEM 12.1.7

A shell is fired with velocity $\mathbf{v}_0$, making a small angle, α_0, with the ground, which is assumed to be a plane. If the air drag is approximated by $|\mathbf{f}| = Kv^2$, where K is constant, determine the trajectory during the interval for which the small-angle assumption is valid.

PROBLEM 12.1.8

A particle moves with constant speed along a horizontal circle on the inner surface of an inverted right circular cone. The axis of the cone is vertical and the half-cone angle is θ. The circular path of the particle is a distance h above the vertex of the cone. What is the speed of the particle? If the motion is perturbed slightly, the particle will oscillate up and down along the wall of the cone. What is the frequency f of this oscillation? Friction is to be neglected.

PROBLEM 12.1.9

A particle is placed on the top of a sphere of radius R. Because of some infinitesimal disturbance, the particle begins to slide down the frictionless surface of the sphere. The sphere is fixed on a horizontal plane. Find the angle θ when the particle leaves the sphere and the distance $\overline{OA}$, where A is the point at which the particle hits the plane and O the point of contact of the sphere.

PROBLEM 12.1.10

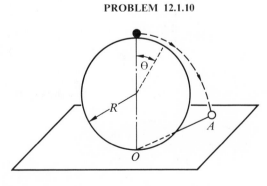

PROBLEM 12.1.11

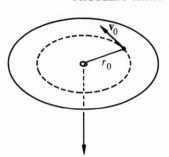

A particle of mass m is attached to a string of negligible mass. Initially, the particle moves in a circular path of radius r_0 on a frictionless horizontal plate with constant speed v_0. The particle is then slowly pulled toward the center of the circle. Show that the angular momentum of the particle is conserved. Assume that $\ddot{r} \ll v^2/r$ and $\dot{r} \ll v$.

PROBLEM 12.1.12

A particle of mass m is released from rest at point A on a frictionless surface. If the radius of curvature at point B is 10 ft, what is the force exerted by the surface on the particle when it reaches B? What is the minimum value of the radius of curvature at point C so that the particle will not leave the surface?

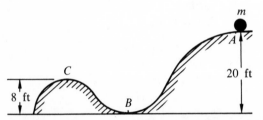

Section 12.2 Motion of a system

SAMPLE PROBLEM

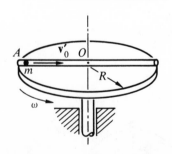

A uniform circular platform of mass M and radius R rotates about the vertical axis with constant angular velocity ω. A tube of negligible mass is attached to the platform as shown. A particle of mass m is fired from A with an initial velocity v_0 relative to the tube. Assume that the particle moves along the axis of the tube, which exerts a friction force of constant magnitude, f, on the particle. Determine the torque $\mathbf{M}$ required to keep the angular velocity of the platform constant. Neglect friction in the bearing.

Solution

Fix the coordinate system xyz in the disk

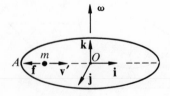

$$\mathbf{r} = x\mathbf{i} \qquad \boldsymbol{\omega} = \omega\mathbf{k}$$

$$\mathbf{v}' = \dot{x}\mathbf{i} \qquad \mathbf{f} = -f\mathbf{i} \text{ for } \dot{x} > 0$$

$$\mathbf{a}' = \ddot{x}\mathbf{i}$$

Methods of dynamics in space

$$a = a' + \omega \times v' + \omega \times (\omega \times r)$$

$$\omega \times v' = \dot{x}\omega j$$

$$\omega \times r = x\omega j$$

$$\omega \times (\omega \times r) = -x\omega^2 i$$

$$F = ma: \qquad -f = m(\ddot{x} - x\omega^2)$$

$$\ddot{x} = \dot{x}\frac{d\dot{x}}{dx}$$

that is,
$$\left(\omega^2 x - \frac{f}{m}\right) dx = \dot{x}\, d\dot{x}$$

$$\left(\frac{1}{2}\omega^2 x^2 - \frac{f}{m}x\right) + \frac{1}{2}C = \frac{1}{2}\dot{x}^2$$

where C is a constant of integration.

At $x = -R$, $\dot{x} = v_0'$: $C = v_0'^2 - \omega^2 R^2 - (2fR)/m$

so that

$$\dot{x} = \left(v_0'^2 - \omega^2 R^2 - 2\frac{f}{m}R + \omega^2 x^2 - 2\frac{f}{m}x\right)^{1/2} \qquad (1)$$

$$\frac{dh}{dt} = M:$$

$$h = h_{disk} + r \times mv$$

$$v = v' + \omega \times r = \dot{x}i + x\omega j$$

$$r \times mv = mx^2\omega k$$

$$\frac{dh}{dt} = 2mx\dot{x}\omega k = M \qquad (2)$$

Using (1) we have M as a function of position coordinate x.

Two particles of mass 0.1 slug each slide along AO and OB, respectively. Rod AOB is perpendicular to rod OC, which rotates in a frictionless bearing at constant angular speed $\omega = 10$ radians/sec. At a certain instant, the particles, both located 3 ft from point O, move outward at 5 ft/sec relative to the rods. Calculate the kinetic energy and angular momentum of the particles and the moment required to maintain constant angular speed at this instant.

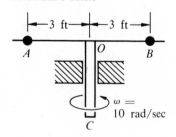

PROBLEM 12.2.2

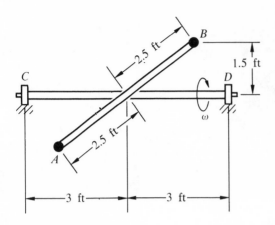

Rod *AB* is rigidly attached to shaft *CD*, which rotates in bearings *C* and *D* at constant angular speed $\omega = 5$ radians/sec. Concentrated masses of 0.1 slug each are attached to the rod at its ends. Neglecting the mass of the rod and shaft, find the maximum and minimum vertical reactions in the bearings due to rotation. Use the principle of angular momentum.

PROBLEM 12.2.3

A simple pendulum of length *l* and mass *m* is attached to link *OA*, of length *a*, which rotates at constant angular speed *ω*. When the pendulum is deflected, it will oscillate about the radial direction. Find the frequency of this oscillation for small values of θ. The device remains in the horizontal plane.

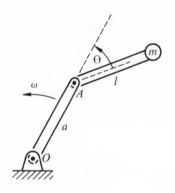

PROBLEM 12.2.4

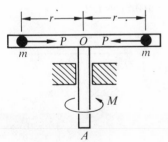

The particles, each of mass *m*, slide in a frictionless tube which turns about axis *OA*, which is perpendicular to the tube. A force of constant magnitude *P* is applied to each of the particles toward the center point *O*. A constant torque *M* is also applied to the shaft *OA*. If the two masses are initially equidistant from point *O*, and the mass of the tube and shaft is neglected, set up the equation of motion for the two particles.

Methods of dynamics in space

Two simple pendulums, *EC* and *FD*, each of mass *m* and length *l*, are attached to shaft *AB*. The suspension points *E* and *F* are located at a distance *e* from the center line of the shaft. At the instant shown, shaft *AB* rotates in the frictionless bearings with angular velocity ω and angular acceleration $\dot{\omega}$, while the arms pivot about pins *E* and *F* each with angular speed $\dot{\theta}$. What is the torque required on the shaft to produce this motion?

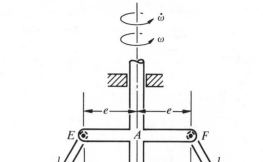

A slender rod of length $L = 4$ ft and mass 0.5 slug is pinned at *B* to a vertical axle *CD* which rotates with a constant angular speed $\omega = 15$ radians/sec. Wire *AE* is attached between the rod and the axle as shown. Determine the tension in the wire.

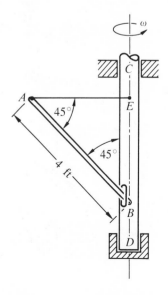

PROBLEM 12.2.7

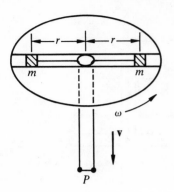

The rotating disk shown has a moment of inertia of 1 slug-ft² about its axis of rotation. The masses, m, are each 0.1 slug and are constrained to move in a groove in the disk. The masses are pulled toward the center of the disk by strings attached to handle P. At the instant when $r = 1$ ft, $v = 6$ in./sec, and $\omega = 4$ radians/sec, what is the angular acceleration of the disk?

PROBLEM 12.2.8

A scoop of mass M_1 is attached to an arm of length L and of negligible mass. The arm is pivoted such that the scoop is free to swing in a vertical arc. The pivot is located at distance L above a pile of sand. The scoop is elevated to a position where the arm makes an angle of 45° with the vertical and is then released. The scoop swings down and picks up a mass of sand, M_2. What is the angle between the arm and the vertical when the scoop reaches its maximum height after picking up the sand? Assume that the sand is picked up instantaneously and friction can be neglected.

PROBLEM 12.2.9

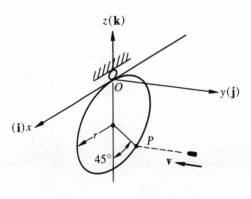

A bullet of mass m is fired with a velocity $\mathbf{v} = -v\mathbf{j}$ into a circular plate of mass M which is supported by a ball joint at O and is initially at rest in the xy-plane. The bullet hits point P and becomes embedded in the plate. Determine the energy lost due to the impact, assuming that $m/M \ll 1$.

Methods of dynamics in space

Section 12.3 Moving frames of reference

At the instant shown, the platform has an angular velocity **n** about the z-axis. The cylinder of radius a has angular velocity **s** and angular acceleration **ṡ** relative to the platform. Particle P slides along a generator of the cylinder with velocity **v** and acceleration **v̇** relative to the cylinder. Determine the absolute velocity and absolute acceleration of the particle when it is located on the top of the cylinder at a distance d from the z-axis.

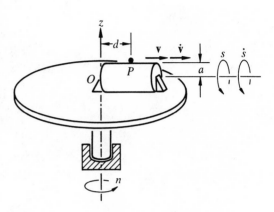

Solution

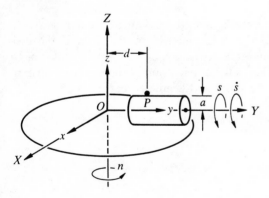

Fix XYZ in space; fix xyz in the cylinder. The angular velocity of the moving frame is

$$\boldsymbol{\Omega} = n\mathbf{K} + s\mathbf{j}$$

$$\dot{\boldsymbol{\Omega}} = \dot{n}\mathbf{K} + n\frac{d\mathbf{K}}{dt} + \dot{s}\mathbf{j} + s\frac{d\mathbf{j}}{dt}$$

$$= \dot{s}\mathbf{j} + s(n\mathbf{K} + s\mathbf{j}) \times \mathbf{j}$$

$$= \dot{s}\mathbf{j} - ns\mathbf{i}$$

$$\mathbf{v}_P = \frac{\delta \mathbf{r}}{\delta t} + \boldsymbol{\Omega} \times \mathbf{r} = v\mathbf{j} + (n\mathbf{K} + s\mathbf{j}) \times (d\mathbf{j} + a\mathbf{k})$$

$$= v\mathbf{j} + \begin{vmatrix} \mathbf{i} & \mathbf{j} & \mathbf{k} \\ O & s & n \\ O & d & a \end{vmatrix} = (sa - dn)\mathbf{i} + v\mathbf{j}$$

$$\mathbf{a}_P = \frac{\delta^2 \mathbf{r}}{\delta t^2} + \frac{\delta \boldsymbol{\Omega}}{\delta t} \times \mathbf{r} + \boldsymbol{\Omega} \times (\boldsymbol{\Omega} \times \mathbf{r}) + 2\boldsymbol{\Omega} \times \frac{\delta \mathbf{r}}{\delta t}$$

$$= \dot{v}\mathbf{j} + \begin{vmatrix} \mathbf{i} & \mathbf{j} & \mathbf{k} \\ -ns & \dot{s} & O \\ O & d & a \end{vmatrix} + \begin{vmatrix} \mathbf{i} & \mathbf{j} & \mathbf{k} \\ O & s & n \\ (sa-dn) & O & O \end{vmatrix}$$

$$+ 2 \begin{vmatrix} \mathbf{i} & \mathbf{j} & \mathbf{k} \\ O & s & n \\ O & v & O \end{vmatrix}$$

$$= (\dot{s}a - 2nv)\mathbf{i} + (\dot{v} + 2ans - dn^2)\mathbf{j} - as^2\,\mathbf{k}$$

PROBLEM 12.3.1 The pin P moves counterclockwise in a circular slot at a constant speed of 1 ft/sec relative to the disk. If the disk accelerates counterclockwise from rest at a rate of 4 radians/sec², what is the acceleration of the pin at the instant the disk reaches a speed of 12 radians/sec?

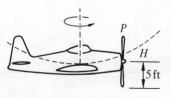

PROBLEM 12.3.2 An airplane flies at 200 mph while simultaneously undergoing a yawing motion of 2 radians/sec about a vertical axis and describing a loop in the vertical plane. The radius of the loop is 1/18 mile. The propeller rotates at 400 rpm about its own axis. Find the velocity of the tip P of the propeller relative to the hub H of the propeller. The length of the propeller blade is 5 ft and it points upward at the instant in question.

Methods of dynamics in space

Find the Coriolis acceleration of an airplane at latitude 30°N and flying north along a meridian with a speed of 500 mph. The radius of the earth is 3,960 miles and its angular velocity is 0.729×10^{-4} radians/sec. Consider the axis of the earth as fixed in space.

PROBLEM 12.3.3

A man stands on the edge of a circular disk which rotates in a horizontal plane with constant angular velocity Ω about the axis through its center. A target is mounted on the opposite end of the diameter which passes through the point where the man stands. If a stone is thrown by the man toward the target, will the stone hit the target? Prove your answer. Neglect gravitational force and air friction.

PROBLEM 12.3.4

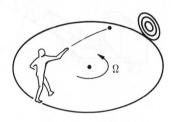

If, in Prob. 12.3.4, the stone was thrown with an initial velocity having a horizontal component relative to the disk at an angle of 45° to the diameter passing through the man and the target, determine the initial velocity **v** relative to the disk necessary for the stone to hit the target. Include gravitational force, but neglect air friction. The radius of the disk is $R = 10$ ft; its angular speed is $\Omega = 1$ radian/sec.

PROBLEM 12.3.5

Shaft D rotates about axis AA at a constant angular speed of 10 rpm. Shaft E rotates about axis CC, which is perpendicular to AA, with a constant angular speed of 10 rpm. Disk F rotates about axis BB, which is perpendicular to CC, at a constant angular speed of 5 rpm. At a certain instant line BB is perpendicular to line AA. Find the acceleration of the highest point, P, on disk F. $\overline{OO'} = 40$ ft, $\overline{O'P} = 3$ ft.

PROBLEM 12.3.6

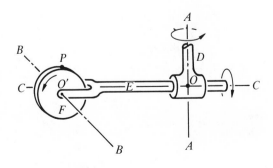

PROBLEM 12.3.7

A crane rotates about the y-axis at constant angular speed $\Omega = 1$ radian/sec. The lifting arm is being raised at a constant angular speed $\omega = 1$ radian/sec. If $OP = 40$ ft, determine the velocity and acceleration of point P when $\theta = 30°$.

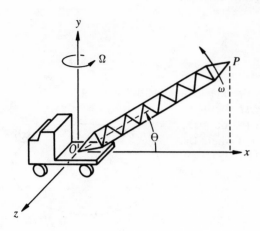

PROBLEM 12.3.8   A car is driven at constant speed v around a level curve of constant curvature K. What is the instantaneous acceleration of the highest point of a tire of radius R?

PROBLEM 12.3.9   An insect runs at constant relative speed v around the rim of a wheel of radius a, which rolls along a straight track at constant speed V. Find the acceleration of the insect at any instant in terms of its position on the wheel.

Methods of dynamics in space

Section 12.4   Motion of a rigid body

A uniform circular disk of radius 2 ft and weight 32.2 lb is mounted as shown on a rotating shaft of negligible mass. At the instant shown, the angular velocity $\omega = 10$ radians/sec and $\dot{\omega} = 8$ radians/sec², both in the same direction. What are the dynamic bearing reactions at this instant?

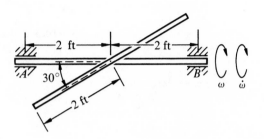

Solution

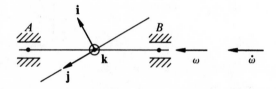

Let **i j k** be principal axes fixed in disk:

$$I_{xx} = I_{yy} + I_{zz} = 4 \text{ slug-ft}^2$$

$$I_{yy} = I_{zz} = 2 \text{ slug-ft}^2$$

$$\omega_x = \omega \sin 30° = 5 \text{ radians/sec}$$

$$\omega_y = \omega \cos 30° = 8.66 \text{ radians/sec}$$

$$\omega_z = 0$$

$$\dot{\omega}_x = \dot{\omega} \sin 30° = 4 \text{ radians/sec}^2$$

$$\dot{\omega}_y = \dot{\omega} \cos 30° = 6.93 \text{ radians/sec}^2$$

$$\dot{\omega}_z = 0$$

From the Euler equations:

$$M_x = I_{xx}\dot{\omega}_x + \omega_y\omega_z(I_{zz} - I_{yy}) = 16 \text{ lb-ft}$$

$$M_y = I_{yy}\dot{\omega}_y + \omega_x\omega_z(I_{xx} - I_{zz}) = 13.86 \text{ lb-ft}$$

$$M_z = I_{zz}\dot{\omega}_z + \omega_x\omega_y(I_{yy} - I_{xx}) = -86.6 \text{ lb-ft}$$

$\mathbf{M} = M_x\mathbf{i} + M_y\mathbf{j} + M_z\mathbf{k}$ is the total moment exerted by the bearings on the shaft due to rotation.

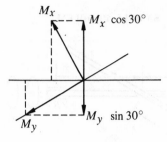

The total moment has two components normal to the shaft; namely,

$$M_x \cos 30° - M_y \sin 30° = 5.92 \text{ lb-ft}$$

and
$$M_z = -86.6 \text{ lb-ft}$$

so that, taking moments about each bearing, we get the dynamic bearing reactions:

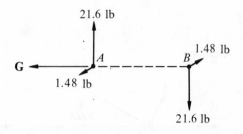

In addition, there is an axial couple of magnitude

$$G = M_x \sin 30° + M_y \cos 30° = 20.80 \text{ lb-ft}$$

PROBLEM 12.4.1 A uniform square plate is rotating about instantaneous axis AA with an angular velocity ω when corner P is suddenly fixed. What is the new angular velocity ω'?

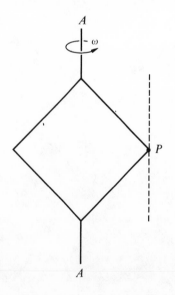

Methods of dynamics in space

A uniform bar of length L and mass M is hinged at end O such that it can rotate about a horizontal axis passing through O. The bar is released from rest at position θ_0. Find the angular velocity of the bar as a function of θ. Neglect friction.

PROBLEM 12.4.2

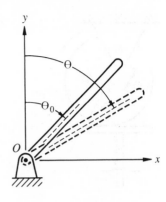

Gear A of radius a and mass M is mounted on shaft AO of length L. Shaft AO is attached to vertical shaft OD by a clevis. Shaft OD turns with constant angular velocity ω while gear A rolls on fixed gear B of radius b. Assuming that gear A is equivalent to a thin disk and the mass of $\overline{AO}$ is negligible, find the maximum value of ω for which the two gears remain in contact.

PROBLEM 12.4.3

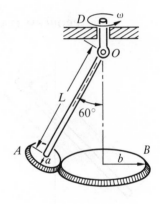

Two particles of mass m and $2m$, respectively, are connected by a bar of negligible mass and of length l. The system is initially at rest in the xy-plane as shown. A force $\mathbf{F}$ of constant magnitude is applied to mass m such that $\mathbf{F}$ lies in the xy-plane and is always normal to the bar. Find the angular velocity and the angular displacement of the bar after the force has been applied for time t.

PROBLEM 12.4.4

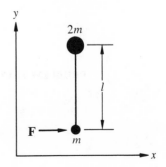

Motion of a rigid body   223

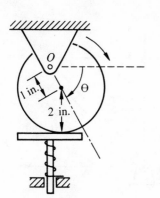

PROBLEM 12.4.5 A circular cam with a radius of 2 in. and an eccentricity of 1 in. rotates at a constant angular speed of 500 rpm about a horizontal shaft passing through O. The cam controls the vertical motion of a 2-lb cam follower held against the cam by a spring. The spring has a constant of 18 lb/in. and is compressed 1 in. when $\theta = 0$. What is the normal force N exerted by the cam on the follower as a function of angle θ? Neglect friction.

PROBLEM 12.4.6 A uniform bar of length L and mass M rotates with constant angular velocity ω about a vertical axis passing through point O as shown. Use the Euler equations of motion to determine the value of θ.

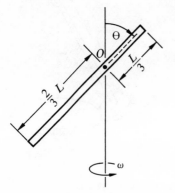

PROBLEM 12.4.7 A uniform bar of length l and mass M initially stands vertically on a frictionless horizontal plane. Because of an infinitesimal disturbance, the bar begins to fall. Set up the differential equations of motion in terms of the angle of inclination θ and the position of the mass center x_0, and determine the path of the mass center during the fall.

224

Methods of dynamics in space

A uniform bar of mass M and length l is released from rest when $\theta = \theta_0$. The wall and floor are frictionless, and the bar moves in a plane perpendicular to both. Find the angular velocity of the bar as a function of θ.

PROBLEM 12.4.8

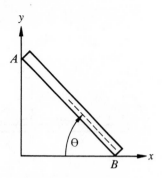

Determine the value of angle θ in Prob. 12.4.8 when the bar leaves the vertical wall.

PROBLEM 12.4.9

The uniform circular disk shown is mounted on a shaft such that a normal to the disk makes an angle of 60° with the shaft. The weight of the disk is 64.4 lb and its radius is 2 ft. If the shaft, which is assumed to have negligible mass, rotates at 60 rpm, what are the total vertical bearing reactions as a function of position at A and B, which are 6 ft apart?

PROBLEM 12.4.10

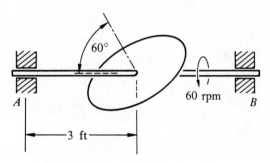

A solid homogeneous right circular cone of height b and semivertex angle α rolls on a horizontal plane without slipping. The line of contact rotates about the z-axis at constant angular velocity Ω. Prove that the maximum value of Ω for the cone to remain in contact with the plane is

$$\frac{1}{2k \cos \alpha} [gb(1 + 3 \sin^2 \alpha) \sin \alpha]^{\frac{1}{2}}$$

where k is the radius of gyration of the cone about a slant height.

PROBLEM 12.4.11

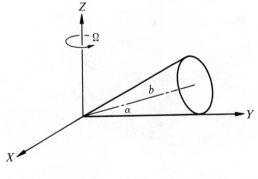

Motion of a rigid body

225

PROBLEM 12.4.12

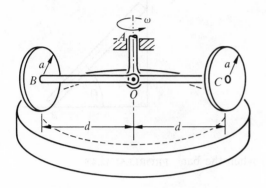

A grinder consists of two uniform disks, each of mass m and radius a, as shown. At point O, a pin in shaft OA permits motion of arms OB and OC in the vertical plane. Shaft OA rotates with constant angular velocity ω. The disks roll on the base without slipping. Determine the normal force exerted on the base by each disk, neglecting the mass of the shafts.

PROBLEM 12.4.13

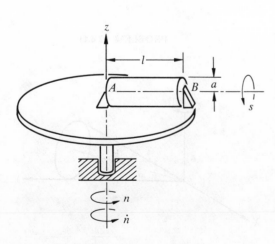

At the instant shown, the platform has angular velocity $\mathbf{n}$ and angular acceleration $\dot{\mathbf{n}}$ about the vertical z-axis. The uniform right circular cylinder of mass m, radius a, and length l has constant angular velocity $\mathbf{s}$ about shaft AB, which is mounted in a journal bearing at A and a thrust bearing at B. Determine the forces exerted on the cylinder at the bearings.

Methods of dynamics in space

Section 12.5 Impulsive motion

Two gears of pitch radii r_1 and r_2, and centroidal moments of inertia I_1 and I_2, respectively, rotate in the counterclockwise direction in frictionless bearings on parallel axes as shown. Their initial angular speeds are ω_1 and ω_2, respectively. The gears are now meshed. Compute the directions and magnitudes ω_1' and ω_2' of their angular velocities after the gears have been engaged.

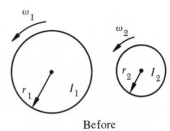

Before

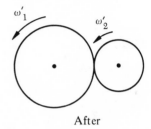

After

Solution

Free-body diagram during meshing:

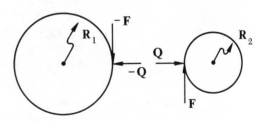

Let Δt be the small time interval during which the gears become engaged. By integration of the moment equation we obtain

$$-\int_0^{\Delta t} Fr_1 \, dt = I_1(\omega_1' - \omega_1)$$

$$-\int_0^{\Delta t} Fr_2 \, dt = I_2(\omega_2' - \omega_2)$$

Since r_1 and r_2 are time-independent during the brief time interval Δt, we obtain

Impulsive motion   227

$$\frac{r_2}{r_1} = \frac{I_2}{I_1} \frac{(\omega_2' - \omega_2)}{(\omega_1' - \omega_1)} \tag{1}$$

Also, after engagement of the gears, the contact points must have equal velocities; hence

$$r_1\omega_1' = -r_2\omega_2' \tag{2}$$

From (1) and (2) we may solve for ω_1' and ω_2':

$$r_1\omega_1' = -r_2\omega_2' = \frac{\dfrac{I_1\omega_1}{r_1} - \dfrac{I_2\omega_2}{r_2}}{\dfrac{I_1}{r_1{}^2} + \dfrac{I_2}{r_2{}^2}} \tag{3}$$

Thus, if

$$\frac{I_1\omega_1}{r_1} > \frac{I_2\omega_2}{r_2}$$

then it follows from (3) that the first gear continues to rotate in the counterclockwise direction; the second gear now rotates in the clockwise direction.

PROBLEM 12.5.1 An experimental test sled moves with a velocity of 1,000 mph. A droplet of water weighing 0.05 oz is at rest in the path of the sled. High-speed photography shows that the droplet impinges on the surface of the sled and comes to rest relative to the sled at a position 3 in. beyond the point of impact. Find the average force exerted on the sled by the droplet.

PROBLEM 12.5.2 A railroad car weighing 50 tons rests against an uncompressed buffer spring at the end of a siding. The spring constant is 50,000 lb/ft. An identical car rolls down the siding at a speed of 4 ft/sec and couples to the first car such that they move together. What is the time required to attain maximum compression of the spring?

PROBLEM 12.5.3 Two blocks weighing 2 lb and 3 lb, respectively, are connected by a spring with a constant of 12 lb/in. and an unstretched length of 6 in. The system is placed on a frictionless horizontal plane; the spring is compressed 2 in. and then released. Find the velocity of each block when the spring is again at its unstretched length.

228

A 30-ft iron chain weighing 300 lb is held over a platform such that the lower end just touches the platform. If the chain is released, find the total impulse imparted during (a) the first sec and (b) the first 2 sec. Assume that the impact is plastic and the platform moves as the chain falls such that the links do not pile up on one another.

PROBLEM 12.5.4

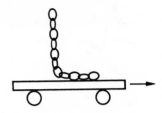

A rectangular plate with sides of length $2a$ and $2b$, respectively, is initially at rest in space. An impulsive force is applied at corner A normal to the plate. Prove that the plate will begin to rotate about the line given by $(3x/a) + (3y/b) + 1 = 0$.

PROBLEM 12.5.5

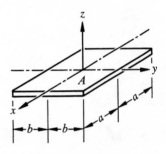

A wheel, which may be assumed to be a homogeneous disk of radius R, rolls with velocity $\mathbf{v}$ along a flat horizontal surface. If the wheel rolls over a depression of width w in the surface and does not bounce or slip at either edge, what is its new velocity after clearing the depression?

PROBLEM 12.5.6

A uniform circular disk of mass M and radius a is mounted at its center O so that it can rotate about any axis passing through O. The disk initially rotates with constant angular velocity ω_0 about the axis normal to the disk. A particle of mass m strikes the edge of the disk with velocity $\mathbf{v}_0$ normal to the disk. If the particle sticks to the disk, find the velocity of the particle immediately after impact.

PROBLEM 12.5.7

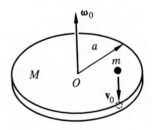

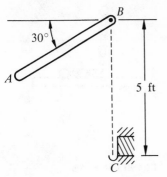

PROBLEM 12.5.8 A uniform rod of length $l = 4$ ft and mass $m = 0.1$ slug is released from rest at an angle of $30°$ with a horizontal plane as shown, and falls under the action of gravity. The eyebolt at end B and the hook at C, which is rigidly mounted, link together after contact.

(a) Determine the velocity of end A immediately after the impact.

(b) Determine the impulsive force applied to the rod.

APPLICATIONS
IN DYNAMICS
IN SPACE: MOTION
OF A PARTICLE

Section 13.2   The simple pendulum

SAMPLE PROBLEM The initial conditions for the motion of a simple pendulum are $\theta = \alpha$ and $\alpha\dot{\theta} = v$. Obtain the relation between position and time in integral form for $0 \leq \theta \leq v/a$.

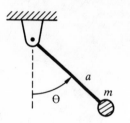

Solution

$$\frac{1}{2} ma^2\dot{\theta}^2 - mga \cos \theta = E = \frac{mv^2}{2} - mga \cos \alpha$$

$$\dot{\theta}^2 = 2 \frac{g}{a} (\cos \theta - \cos \alpha) + \frac{v^2}{a^2}$$

$$= 2p^2 (\cos \theta - \cos \alpha) + q^2$$

where $p^2 = \dfrac{g}{a}$

$$q^2 = \frac{v^2}{a^2}$$

232

CHAPTER 13

$$\dot{\theta} = \sqrt{2p^2(\cos \theta - \cos \alpha) + q^2}$$

$$dt = \frac{d\theta}{\sqrt{2p^2(\cos \theta - \cos \alpha) + q^2}}$$

$$t - t_0 = \int_\alpha^\theta \frac{d\theta'}{\sqrt{2p^2(\cos \theta' - \cos \alpha) + q^2}}$$

The maximum amplitude of a simple pendulum of mass m and length l is 60°. Find the tension in the string as a function of the inclination of angle θ.

PROBLEM 13.2.1

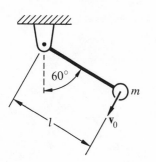

PROBLEM 13.2.2 A simple pendulum is made of a light string of length l and a bob of mass m. The pendulum is initially held at an angle of $60°$ from the vertical. A tangential velocity $\mathbf{v}$ is imparted to the bob when the string is released. Find the range of values of v for which the bob will stay in a circular path. The string does not support compression.

PROBLEM 13.2.3 A simple pendulum of length l moves in a complete circle about its support. Show that the period of one revolution is

$$\frac{4l}{v_0} \int_0^1 \frac{dy}{\left[(1 - y^2)\left(1 - \dfrac{4gly^2}{v_0^{\,2}} \right) \right]^{\frac{1}{2}}}$$

where v_0 is the speed of the bob at the lowest position.

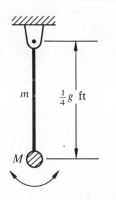

PROBLEM 13.2.4 A pendulum consists of a uniform rod of length $\frac{1}{4}g$ ft and mass m and a bob of mass M. Compute the natural frequency of small oscillations in cps. Compare this value of the natural frequency of small oscillations of the system with that calculated on the basis of negligible rod mass.

$\frac{1}{4}g$ ft

Section 13.3   The spherical pendulum

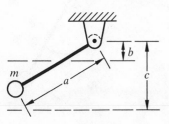

PROBLEM 13.3.1 A spherical pendulum of mass m and length a oscillates between levels b and c, located below the support. Find the expression for the total energy of the system in terms of a, b, c, m, and g, taking the horizontal plane passing through the support as the zero potential level.

234   *Motion of a particle*

A spherical pendulum, consisting of a massless rod and a bob of mass m, is initially held at rest in the horizontal plane. A horizontal velocity v_0 is imparted to the bob normal to the rod. In the resulting motion, what is the angle between the rod and the horizontal plane when the bob is at its lowest position?

PROBLEM 13.3.2

A spherical pendulum of mass m and length a is held such that the string forms an angle $\alpha < (\pi/2)$ with the vertical. A horizontal velocity v_0 is imparted to the bob normal·to the string. Show that the bob will begin to rise if $v_0^2 > ga$ $(\sin^2 \alpha/\cos \alpha)$. Deduce your result from the equations of motion of a spherical pendulum (see Synge and Griffith, p. 337). Discuss the cases of $\alpha = \pi/2$ and $\alpha > \pi/2$.

PROBLEM 13.3.3

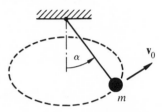

Find the tension in the string of the spherical pendulum in Prob. 13.3.1 when the bob is located at a distance z below the horizontal plane passing through the support.

PROBLEM 13.3.4

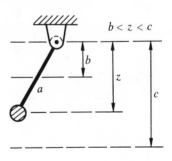

In Prob. 13.3.1, show that the spherical pendulum reduces to a simple pendulum if $c = a$.

PROBLEM 13.3.5

The spherical pendulum

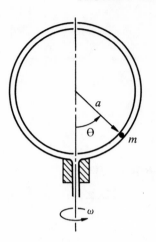

PROBLEM 13.3.6 A particle of mass m is placed inside a frictionless tube of negligible mass. The tube is bent into a circular ring with the lowest point left open as shown. The ring is given an initial angular velocity ω about the vertical axis passing through the diameter containing the opening, and simultaneously the particle is released from rest (relative to the tube) at $\theta = \pi/2$. In the subsequent motion, will the particle drop through the opening?

Section 13.4 The motion of a charged particle in an electromagnetic field

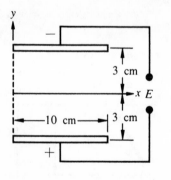

PROBLEM 13.4.1 The voltage in the circuit shown varies according to the relation given on the graph. At time $t = 0$ a hydrogen ion is at $x = 0$, $y = 0$ and has a kinetic energy of 10^{-12} joules. The velocity of the ion at $t = 0$ is along the x-axis. Find the velocity when the particle emerges from the plates and the y-coordinate at that instant. The mass of a hydrogen ion is 1.672×10^{-27} kg.

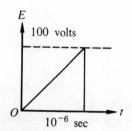

Motion of a particle

An electron is at $x = y = z = 0$ and has zero velocity at time $t = 0$. The electron is subjected to an electromagnetic field given analytically by $\mathbf{E} = E\mathbf{j}$ and $\mathbf{H} = H\mathbf{i}$. Express the coordinates (x,y,z) of the electron as functions of time.

PROBLEM 13.4.2

What is the form of the trajectories of charged particles in an axially symmetrical electric field for which the axial potential is of the form $V_0 = az + b$? [See Eq. (13.429) of Synge and Griffith.]

PROBLEM 13.4.3

Section 13.5 Effects of the earth's rotation

A man aims a gun and fires a bullet with an initial speed of 1,000 ft/sec at a target which is mounted on top of a tower 500 ft high and located 500 ft north of the man. The man is located at a latitude $\lambda = 45°$. Determine the deflection of the bullet at the target due to gravity and the rotation of the earth.

SAMPLE PROBLEM

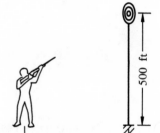

500 ft

500 ft

North

Solution

At $t = 0$, $x = y = z = 0$:

$$\mathbf{v}_0 = 1,000 \left(-\frac{1}{\sqrt{2}}\mathbf{i} + \frac{1}{\sqrt{2}}\mathbf{k} \right) \text{ ft/sec}$$

so that

$$x = u_1 t + \Omega u_2 t^2 \sin \lambda$$

$$y = u_2 t - \Omega t^2 (u_1 \sin \lambda + u_3 \cos \lambda) + \frac{1}{3}\Omega g t^3 \cos \lambda$$

$$z = u_3 t - \frac{1}{2} g t^2 + \Omega u_2 t^2 \cos \lambda$$

where $\qquad \Omega = 7.29 \times 10^5 \text{ radians/sec}$

Effects of the earth's rotation

At $x = -500$ ft:

$$x = -500 = -\frac{1000}{\sqrt{2}}t \qquad t = \frac{\sqrt{2}}{2}\text{ sec}$$

$$y = -\frac{7.29}{10^5}\left(\frac{\sqrt{2}}{2}\right)^2\left(-\frac{1,000}{\sqrt{2}}+\frac{1,000}{\sqrt{2}}\frac{1}{\sqrt{2}}\right)$$

$$+\frac{1}{3}\frac{7.29}{10^5}32.2\left(\frac{\sqrt{2}}{2}\right)^3\frac{1}{\sqrt{2}}$$

$$= 0.000195\text{ ft} = 0.00234\text{ in.}$$

$$z = \frac{1,000}{\sqrt{2}}\frac{\sqrt{2}}{2}-\frac{1}{2}32.2\left(\frac{\sqrt{2}}{2}\right)^2$$

$$= 500 - \frac{1}{2}32.2\frac{2}{4} = (500 - 8.05)\text{ ft}$$

Therefore the deflection is 8.05 ft below and 0.00234 in. to the right.

PROBLEM 13.5.1 A particle is dropped from a vertical distance h (measured radially) above the earth's surface. Find the particle's deflection at impact from the vertical due to the earth's rotation Ω as a function of latitude λ.

PROBLEM 13.5.2 A car of mass M moves southward with a velocity $\mathbf{v}$ and an acceleration $\mathbf{a}$ relative to the earth. Find the total lateral frictional force exerted on the tires as a result of the earth's rotation as a function of latitude λ.

PROBLEM 13.5.3 At latitude 30°N, a bullet is fired toward a target located 3,000 ft north of the firing point. The initial speed of the bullet is 1,000 ft/sec. Find the horizontal deviation due to the earth's rotation neglecting its curvature.

PROBLEM 13.5.4 A projectile is fired vertically upward (i.e., in the direction of the local plumb line). Acknowledging the earth's rotation, will it fall back to its original position? Explain your answer.

Motion of a particle

A locomotive of mass M travels northwest with a constant velocity $\mathbf{v}$ relative to the earth. Find the total force exerted on the track by the locomotive as a function of the latitude λ.

APPLICATIONS IN DYNAMICS IN SPACE: MOTION OF A RIGID BODY

Section 14.1   Motion of a rigid body with a fixed point under no forces

PROBLEM 14.1.1   A bullet is fired such that it has angular velocity ω along an axis making an angle α with its axis of symmetry. Assuming torque-free motion, draw a diagram showing the body and space cones for the case of $C < A = B$, $(A = I_{xx}, B = I_{yy}, C = I_{zz})$. Indicate the direction of the angular momentum vector **H** in the diagram.

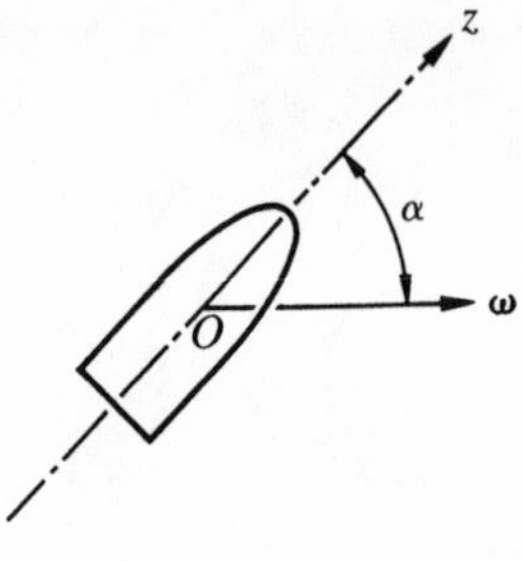

PROBLEM 14.1.2   In Prob. 14.1.1, if $\alpha = 30°$, $A/C = I_{xx}/I_{zz} = 1.5$, and $|\omega| = 10$ radians/sec, what are the spin n about the axis of symmetry and the rate of precession Ω about the invariable line?

PROBLEM 14.1.3   A projectile which has moments of inertia such that $C/A = 1/120$ spins at speed $s = 20\pi$ radians/sec, and precesses such that the angle between the axis of symmetry and the invariable line is $\theta = 5°$. Find the speed of precession Ω and the angle between the resultant velocity vector and the invariable line. Draw the body and space cones.

CHAPTER 14

A uniform circular disk is pivoted at its center O such that it can rotate about any axis passing through O. The disk is set to spin at angular speed $\omega = 10$ radians/sec about an axis making angle $\alpha = 30°$ with the z-axis, which is normal to the disk at O. Find the time required for the z-axis to describe a complete cone in space.

PROBLEM 14.1.4

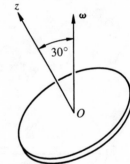

Two identical uniform disks of mass $m/2$ and radius $a = 3$ ft are connected by a weightless rigid rod $AB = 6$ ft. The center point O of the rod is fixed. The system initially spins about axis AB with angular speed $\omega_0 = 60$ rpm. A particle of mass $m' = m/100$ with velocity $v_0 = 7,500$ ft/sec normal to the face of the disks strikes and sticks to the edge of disk B. Find the angular velocity of the system immediately after impact. Determine the axis and rate of precession.

PROBLEM 14.1.5

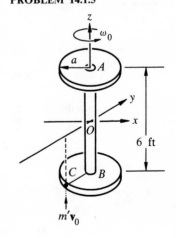

241

PROBLEM 14.1.6

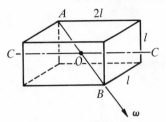

The geometric center O of the block shown is fixed in space. The block rotates about diagonal AB with angular velocity ω. There are no external forces. Find the half-angle α of the body cone. Find the time required for the longitudinal axis of symmetry CC to make one revolution.

PROBLEM 14.1.7

A rigid body with an axis of symmetry has principal moments of inertia A and $B = C = 10A$. The body is attached to a frictionless pivot at its center of mass. The body is initially rotating with angular velocity ω about its axis of symmetry. An impulsive couple $\hat{\mathbf{G}}$ of magnitude $|\hat{\mathbf{G}}| = \frac{1}{10}A\omega$ is now applied to the body along a given line perpendicular to the axis of symmetry. Determine the subsequent precession of the body.

Section 14.2   The spinning top

PROBLEM 14.2.1

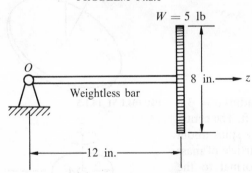

A uniform disk rotates about its center line Oz at a speed of 10,000 rpm. Point O is fixed by a frictionless ball joint. The system is released from a horizontal position. What are the limiting values of the nutation angle?

PROBLEM 14.2.2

A ship's power plant has a turbine rotor weighing 3,220 lb with a radius of gyration of 10 in. The rotor is mounted in two bearings 5 ft apart, with its axis horizontal in the fore-and-aft direction. The center of gravity of the turbine is 3 ft aft of the forward bearing. The turbine rotates at 5,000 rpm counterclockwise when viewed from the stern. Find the vertical components of the bearing reactions when the ship is making a 500-yd port (left) turn at a speed of 20 knots.

Motion of a rigid body

A homogeneous solid of revolution moves such that one point remains fixed. If the motion is such that the angle between the axis of symmetry of the body and the invariable line is constant and equal to twice the angle between angular velocity vector ω and the invariable line, what is the magnitude of the couple necessary to maintain this motion? Express your answer in terms of $|\omega|$ and α, the half-angle of the body cone.

A uniform circular disk has a diameter of 6 in., is 2 in. thick, and has a weight density of 480 lb/ft^3. It spins at an angular speed of 6,000 rpm about axis OA, which is normal to the disk at its center A and fixed at O. Neglecting the mass of shaft OA, determine the precession speed p if the disk is released when OA is horizontal.

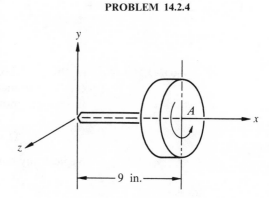

A sleeping top is made of two solid right circular cones as shown. The top spins at speed $s = 150$ radians/sec about axis AB. Is the motion stable? Is it stable if end A is at the bottom?

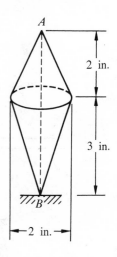

The spinning top

243

PROBLEM 14.2.6

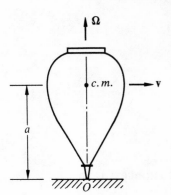

A top spins with an angular velocity Ω about its axis of symmetry which is initially vertical, and it also slides with velocity $\mathbf{v}$ on a frictionless horizontal plane. The contact point strikes a crack at O and is prevented from moving farther. Mass of the top $= m$; $C = \frac{1}{2} ma^2$; $B = A = \frac{5}{4} ma^2$ (about point O). Determine:

(a) The angular velocity of the top immediately after the impact;

(b) The impulsive force exerted on the top;

(c) The energy loss caused by the impact.

PROBLEM 14.2.7

In Prob. 14.2.6, determine the maximum angle between the axis of symmetry of the top and the vertical axis in the subsequent motion, where

$$\Omega = |\Omega| = 10 \sqrt{g/a} \qquad |\mathbf{v}| = \tfrac{1}{10} \Omega a$$

Neglect any couple due to friction at point O.

Section 14.3   Gyroscopes

PROBLEM 14.3.1

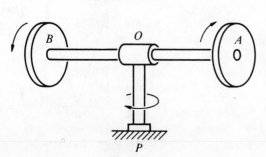

The device shown has two identical disks at A and B which rotate freely in the directions indicated. Shaft OP rotates about a vertical axis. If shaft BOA is flexible, do points A and B move up or down? Neglect the effect of gravity.

Motion of a rigid body

A symmetrical flywheel with transverse and axial moments of inertia A and C spins at great speed s. It oscillates with its center of gravity stationary, subject to restraining moments $k_1\theta$ and $k_2\phi$ exerted by the springs attached to the sleeves. What are the equations of motion?

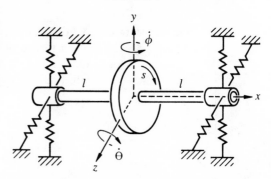

It is desired to utilize a gyrostabilizer to counteract the tendency of an automobile to tip when rounding a corner. The gyro used has weight w and radius of gyration k and is mounted with its axis parallel to the axle of the car. If it is required that the normal force of the road on the tires remain constant as the car rounds a curve, what should the speed and direction of rotation of the gyro be when the car is making an unbanked level turn at speed v? The center of gravity of the car is at distance h above the ground.

Find the frequency of oscillation of a gyrocompass whose disk is 6 in. in diameter, 1 in. thick, weighs 4 lb, and spins at 16,000 rpm
(a) at the Equator;
(b) at the North Pole;
(c) at latitude 40°N.

A gyro of mass m is attached to a string of length l as shown. The gyro spins at speed s and precesses about the vertical axis at constant speed Ω. Write the equations of motion in terms of the axial and transverse moments of inertia C and A.

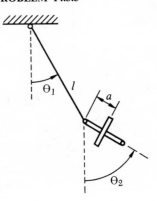

Section 14.4 General motion of a rigid body

PROBLEM 14.4.1 A homogeneous circular cylinder of radius R and weight W has a thread of negligible weight wrapped around its center. One end of the thread is fixed and the cylinder is allowed to fall. Find the acceleration of the center of the cylinder.

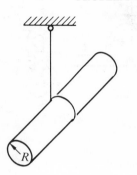

PROBLEM 14.4.2 A uniform rod of length $2a$ and mass M is suspended from a fixed point O by a weightless string of length b. Show that the equations of motion for small oscillations about the vertical are

$$b\frac{d^2l}{dt^2} + a\frac{d^2p}{dt^2} = -\frac{Tl}{M}$$

$$b\frac{d^2m}{dt^2} + a\frac{d^2q}{dt^2} = -\frac{Tm}{M}$$

$$T - Mg = 0$$

where (l,m,n) are the direction cosines of the string and (p,q,r) are the direction cosines of the rod with respect to the set of axes shown. T is the tension in the string.

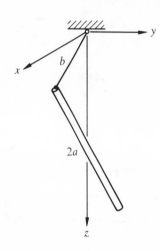

PROBLEM 14.4.3 A homogeneous circular cylinder rests upon a flat slab which is given a constant acceleration of magnitude $a = 2g$. Find the angular acceleration of the cylinder when the coefficient of sliding friction f between the cylinder and the slab equals (a) 0.5, and (b) 0.75.

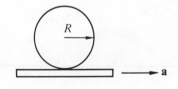

Motion of a rigid body

A uniform disk of mass $m = 1$ slug and radius $a = 1$ ft rolls in a vertical plane up a slope with inclination angle $\theta = 3°$. At point O, the center of the disk has a speed $v_0 = 6$ ft/sec. Determine the distance from O to P, where P is the point beyond which the motion is unstable.

PROBLEM 14.4.4

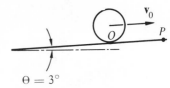

A billiard ball of mass $m = 0.1$ slug and radius $a = 1$ in. is struck such that the center of the ball has a velocity $\mathbf{v}_0 = 1\mathbf{i}$ ft/sec and an angular velocity $\boldsymbol{\omega}_0 = (-12\mathbf{i} + 12\mathbf{j} + 3\mathbf{k})$ radians/sec. The coefficient of kinetic friction between the ball and the table is $\mu = 0.1$. Determine the position and time after impact when slipping ceases. Find the equation for the path of the center of the ball before and after slipping ceases.

PROBLEM 14.4.5

A uniform circular cylinder of mass $m = 1$ slug and radius $a = 1$ ft is given an initial angular speed $\omega = 2$ radians/sec about its axis, which is horizontal. The cylinder is then gently placed on a board of mass $M = 2$ slugs which rests on a smooth table. The coefficient of friction between the cylinder and the board is $\mu = 0.01$. Determine the subsequent motion of the cylinder and of the board. Calculate the kinetic energy lost by the system and the work done by the friction forces up to the instant when the motion becomes uniform.

PROBLEM 14.4.6

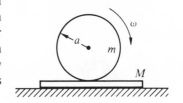

The door of a car is left open when the car starts to move from rest with a constant acceleration $\mathbf{a}$. Assuming that the door can be considered to be a uniform rectangular plate of mass M, determine the angular motion of the door.

PROBLEM 14.4.7

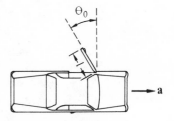